The media's watch
Here's a sampling

M000209052

. . . .

"For those hoping to climb the ladder of success, [Vault's] insights are priceless."
– *Money*

"The best place on the web to prepare for a job search."
– *Fortune*

"[Vault guides] make for excellent starting points for job hunters and should be purchased by academic libraries for their career sections [and] university career centers."
– *Library Journal*

"The granddaddy of worker sites."
– *The U.S. News and World Report*

"A killer app."
– *The New York Times*

One of Forbes' 33 "Favorite Sites"
– *Forbes*

"To get the unvarnished scoop, check out Vault."
– *Smart Money Magazine*

"Vault has a wealth of information about major employers and job-searching strategies as well as comments from workers about their experiences at specific companies."
– *The Washington Post*

"Vault has become the go-to source for career preparation."
– *Crain's New York Business*

"Vault [provides] the skinny on working conditions at all kinds of companies from current and former employees."
– *USA Today*

VAULT
> the most trusted name in career information™

VAULT GUIDE TO THE TOP
PRIVATE EQUITY EMPLOYERS

Use the Internet's
MOST TARGETED
job search tools.

Vault Job Board

Target your search by industry, function, and experience level, and find the job openings that you want.

VaultMatch Resume Database

Vault takes match-making to the next level: post your resume and customize your search by industry, function, experience and more. We'll match job listings with your interests and criteria and e-mail them directly to your inbox.

VAULT GUIDE TO THE TOP
PRIVATE EQUITY
EMPLOYERS

**EDITED BY DEREK LOOSVELT
AND THE STAFF OF VAULT**

Library of Congress CIP Data is available.

ISBN-13 978-1-58131-435-9

ISBN 1-58131-435-3

Printed in the United States of America

ACKNOWLEDGMENTS

We are extremely grateful to Vault's entire staff for all their help in the editorial, production and marketing processes. Vault also would like to acknowledge the support of our investors, clients, employees, family and friends. Thank you!

Table of Contents

Visit Vault at **www.vault.com** for insider company profiles, expert advice,
career message boards, expert resume reviews, the Vault Job Board and more.

V/\ULT CAREER LIBRARY   ix

Introduction

Out of the gate

As its name implies, a private equity firm invests in assets not freely traded on public stock exchanges. Private equity investments can take many shapes; the most well-known is the buyout, a term popularized by Bryan Burroughs and John Helyar's 1989 book *Barbarians at the Gate*, later made into a television movie, following the battle for control of RJR Nabisco. The battle was ultimately won by legendary private equity firm Kohlbergh Kravis Roberts & Co., better known as KKR.

A buyout refers to the purchase of a controlling interest in a company or business unit. A leveraged buyout, commonly referred to as an LBO, which KKR implemented to acquire RJR, is a takeover that uses a significant amount of borrowed money. Other types of private equity investments include mezzanine financing and venture capital. Mezzanine financing uses subordinated debt along with equity to invest in a company, typically prior to an initial public offering. Venture capital, considered a subset of private equity (see the *Vault Career Guide to Venture Capital*), refers to investments in the launch or early development of a company. As opposed to venture capital firms, private equity firms invest in later-stage companies.

Although private equity is a relatively young business – the first of today's large private equity firms, Warburg Pincus, was founded in the late 1960s - now there are more than 2,700 such companies worldwide. In addition to KKR and Warburg, other large players include the Blackstone Group, Texas Pacific Group and the Carlyle Group. (Like KKR, Carlyle was also featured in a mainstream film, receiving air time in Michael Moore's 2004 documentary *Fahrenheit 9/11* for its connections to former President George H. W. Bush and various Saudi investors, including the bin Laden family.) Leading investment banks such as Goldman Sachs, Lehman Brothers and JPMorgan Chase also have private equity units that are now huge players in the industry.

Rockefellers to rock stars

Until the 1970s, private equity investing generally involved wealthy families such as the Rockefellers buying stock in private companies in order to later sell those shares at a higher price. These investments were also largely of the venture capital kind, placed into young firms. Today, though, less than 20 percent of all private equity investments qualify as venture capital, and the

Visit Vault at **www.vault.com** for insider company profiles, expert advice, career message boards, expert resume reviews, the Vault Job Board and more.

VAULT CAREER LIBRARY

1

average private equity fund has ballooned in size. Back in 1980, KKR held claim to the largest fund in the world, with a $135 million pool of cash, raised from institutional investors and wealthy individuals, to make private investments. Currently, numerous funds have more than $1 billion in total capital, and the largest fund to date, held by the Carlyle Group, is $7.8 billion. JP Morgan Partners has a fund that's not far behind, at $6.5 billion, and Blackstone's largest fund comes to $6.4 billion.

In addition to larger funds, another development in recent years is the entrance of the celebrity employee. High-profile names currently working for private equity firms include former General Electric CEO Jack Welch, of Clayton, Dubliler & Rice; former chairman and CEO of IBM Lou Gerstner, now the chairman of the Carlyle Group; and former chairman of the SEC Arthur Levitt, who also works for Carlyle. Other famous folks in the industry include U2 frontman Bono, who recently helped start a private equity firm focusing on media investments, and former U.S. Vice President Dan Quayle, the current chairman of Cerberus Capital Management's advisory board.

Show me the exit

At the beginning of the new millennium, private equity firms lost billions of dollars when the tech bubble burst, sending funding from approximately $300 billion in 2000 down to a low of $93 billion in 2003. However, just as most areas of the financial services sector suffered and then bounced back, private equity investment dollars are now plentiful again, as institutional investors are flowing money back into private equity funds. According to Thomson Venture Economics and the National Venture Capital Association, in the first quarter of 2005, 38 private equity (buyout and mezzanine) funds attracted $15.8 billion, a significant rise from the $3.4 billion that 25 funds raised during the same period a year earlier. During the second quarter of 2005, the numbers were even better, as 38 funds brought in $22.1 billion in commitments, a 32.5 percent increase over the second quarter of 2004. It was also the highest commitment size in a quarter since 2000.

Private equity firms raise money for funds from entities such as pension funds, endowments, corporations and wealthy individuals. Funds are typically set up as limited partnership, thus the LP at the end of most of their names, as in JPMorgan Partners Global Investors, LP. Investors in the funds act as limited partners, a private equity firm as general partner. First, a private equity firm will spend time raising money for a fund. Once it hits a certain amount, it will then announce a first "closing" and begin looking for deals. It could take several years to invest all the money in a fund, and a private equity firm might raise more money in a fund after the first closing. Only when a firm announces a fund's final closing is it no longer open to new investors.

The businesses that a private equity firm purchases with money from its funds are referred to as its "portfolio companies." The Blackstone Group has an equity stake in some 40 portfolio companies, which, according to *The Economist*, together have over 300,000 employees and annual revenue of more than $50 billion. If combined as a single entity, these companies would make Blackstone one of the top 20 Fortune 500 firms. In comparison, Texas Pacific Group's portfolio companies have over 255,000 employees and revenue of $41 billion, while Carlyle's portfolio companies have 150,000 employees and revenue of $31 billion.

Private equity firms make money two ways: either selling their stakes in portfolio companies to corporate buyers at higher prices, or floating their stakes on the public market through IPOs. These two avenues are commonly referred to as "exit strategies." As business owners, private equity firms can increase the value of their investments in several ways. One, and perhaps the most obvious way, is to increase a company's profitability. Another is simply holding onto a company until it falls back in favor with investors or the market. A third is to break up a company into separate units and sell them individually; often, the sum of the values of each unit is higher than their value as a combined entity.

Private equity firms also make money through annual management fees, commonly 1 to 2 percent of the total amount of a fund. Fees are charged to the fund's investors (the limited partners). So, for example, if a firm has raised a $1 billion fund, it might pocket $20 million in management fees each year from its limited partners.

The club and the international

Firms are increasingly sharing portfolio companies, as joint purchases or "club deals" become more common. For example, in August 2005, Silver Lake Partners led a consortium comprised of KKR, Bain Capital, Blackstone, Goldman Sachs Capital Partners, Providence Equity Partners and Texas Pacific to acquire SunGard Data Systems for $11.3 billion. It was the largest tech buyout ever completed. Also in August, KKR teamed up with Silver Lake to purchase Agilent's semiconductor business for $2.65 billion. More recently, in September 2005, the Carlyle Group joined forces with Clayton, Dubilier & Rice and Merrill Lynch Global Private Equity to acquire vehicle rental group Hertz from Ford Motor Company for $15 billion, beating out other private equity groups vying for the investment.

Visit Vault at **www.vault.com** for insider company profiles, expert advice, career message boards, expert resume reviews, the Vault Job Board and more.

VAULT CAREER LIBRARY

3

In addition, private equity firms are more frequently going abroad to find deals, buying and investing in foreign-based companies. Washington D.C.-based Carlyle's recent buys include a $400 million investment in Shanghai's China Pacific Life Insurance Co. and a 60 percent stake in the $2.1 billion takeover of Japanese cell-phone maker DDI Pocket. As of February 2005, Carlyle had invested $4 billion in Asian companies. It currently has a $750 million fund focused on Korea, China and Taiwan, and has plans to raise a $1.25 to $1.5 billion fund for further Asian investments. Among Carlyle's 24 offices worldwide are outposts in Beijing and Mumbia, which both opened in the second half of 2005.

Europe has also become a hot bed for private equity investments. In 2004, private equity groups invested $156 billion in European companies, up 66 percent from 2000. One of the bigger players in the region is New York-based Clayton, Dubilier & Rice, which in March 2005 completed a $4.5 billion buyout of French electrical equipment supplier Rexel, the third largest private equity buyout in Europe to date.

EMPLOYER PROFILES

Advent International Corporation

75 State Street
Boston, MA 02109
Phone: (617) 951-9400
Fax: (617) 951-0566
www.adventinternational.com

THE STATS

Chairman: Peter A. Brooke
Employer Type: Private Company
No. of Employees: 100
No. of Offices: 14

KEY COMPETITORS

Bain Capital
Berkshire Partners
Summit Partners

EMPLOYMENT CONTACT

Boston office/U.S.
Phone: (617) 951-9400
E-mail: info@adventinternational.com
For other offices, see "contact us" at
www.adventinternational.com

THE SCOOP

International investment

Boston-based Advent International is truly an international private equity firm. While most of the big names in private equity have outposts in Europe and Asia, Advent takes "international" to another level, with 14 offices around the world, from Argentina to Southeast Asia. Advent is also responsible for a number of firsts in the global private equity landscape, including putting together the first leveraged buyout in Hungary and Poland, the first private equity-backed public-to-private deal in Central Europe and Spain, and the first global private equity fund (in 1987). Founded in 1984, the firm has backed more than 500 companies in some 35 countries.

Middle of the road

Advent invests in middle-market companies in five core sectors: business and financial services; retail and consumer; health care; technology, media and telecom; and industrial. In North America and Europe, the typical Advent investment is $20 to $200 million; in Central Europe and Latin America, the average outlay is on the smaller end of the range: between $20 million and $60 million. Advent also manages venture capital funds focused on start-up to revenue-stage companies, primarily in North America. The firm's venture investments usually run from $5 million to $20 million.

Deal-making

Advent has been on a shopping spree as of late. In January 2005, the firm brought in the new year with the acquisition of Proservvi, the leading provider of back-office processing services to financial institutions in Brazil. Then in April, Advent bought a stake in Fat Face, the active casual wear market leader in the U.K. One month later, across the Atlantic, the private equity group picked up Making Memories, the Utah-based provider of scrapbook and card-making products. In June, Advent invested in the drilling services and equipment company Boart Longyear and Italian vending machine operator Gruppo Argenta. In August, the global private equity acquired five different companies, ranging from a Romanian paints business to a technology company in the U.K. Most recently, in September 2005, Advent bought a majority stake in Casa Reha, a German private nursing home group.

Visit Vault at **www.vault.com** for insider company profiles, expert advice, career message boards, expert resume reviews, the Vault Job Board and more.

VAULT CAREER LIBRARY

7

GETTING HIRED

Advent International has around 100 investment professionals working out of 14 offices around the world. Although the firm does not offer employment information on its web site, it does provide contact details for each of its outposts. Candidates interested in working for Advent should get in touch with the appropriate office (see "contact us" at www.adventinternational.com).

Allied Capital Corporation

1919 Pennsylvania Ave. NW
Washington, D.C. 20006-3434
Phone: (202) 331-1112
Fax: (202) 659-2053
www.alliedcapital.com

THE STATS

Chairman & CEO: William L. Walton
Employer Type: Public Company
Ticker Symbol: ALD (NYSE)
Revenue: $415.6 milloin
Net Income: $249.5 million
No. of Employees: 162
No. of Offices: 4

KEY COMPETITORS

American Capital Strategies
CapitalSource
CIT Group

EMPLOYMENT CONTACT

jobs@alliedcapital.com

THE SCOOP

Mezzanine masters

Allied Capital is a type of private equity firm known as a business development company or BDC (a buyout firm that goes public and sells shares in itself). In the case of Allied Capital, the capital raised from shareholders is used to fund mezzanine and equity investments in small and middle-market companies. Founded in 1958, Allied Capital pioneered the mezzanine finance business (capital raised before a company goes public) and has financed thousands of companies in its nearly 50 years in the business. In 2004, Allied Capital was named "Middle Market Financing Firm of the Year" by publishing firm M&A Advisor. Based in Washington, D.C., Allied has additional offices in New York, Chicago and Los Angeles.

Targeted investments

Allied Capital invests in companies in a number of different industries, but focuses its energies on five key sectors: business services, financial services, consumer products, energy services and health care services. Within these industries, the firm looks for targets with strong management teams who own significant equity stakes in their companies, a leading market position, steady operating margins, free cash flow; high return on invested capital, and a strong balance sheet. Once Allied Capital invests in a company, it plans to stick around for a while: typical investments last five to 10 years.

Polyethylene and Pets

Allied Capital's recent acquisitions run the gamut from polyethylene to pets. In July 2005, the firm invested $162 million to finance a management-led recapitalization of Norwesco, Inc., a manufacturer of polyethylene tanks to the agricultural and septic tank markets. It also put $40 million in N.E.W. Customer Service Companies, a provider of extended service contracts and buyer protection programs. In August, the private equity group invested $57.1 million in Graham Partners' buyout of Line-X, Inc., a franchisor of branded spray-on pick-up truck bedliners (apparently a common truck accessory). And in September 2005, Allied Capital invested $64.4 million in the buyout of Healthy Pet Corp., an operator of veterinary hospitals in the U.S.

GETTING HIRED

Allied Capital doesn't have much information on its career page – but, unlike many private equity firms, at least it has one. The firm says it's looking for candidates who are "articulate and achievement-oriented, and possess a high degree of integrity, strong interpersonal and partnership skills, and intellectual curiosity." Most professionals work out of the firm's headquarters in Washington, D.C., but positions are also available at the firm's satellite offices. Interested individuals should submit their resume to jobs@alliedcapital.com.

Visit Vault at **www.vault.com** for insider company profiles, expert advice,
career message boards, expert resume reviews, the Vault Job Board and more.

VAULT CAREER LIBRARY

11

American Capital Strategies, Ltd.

2 Bethesda Metro Center
14th Floor
Bethesda, MD 20814
Phone: (301) 951-6122
Fax: (301) 654-6714
www.american-capital.com

THE STATS

Chairman & CEO: Malon Wilkus
Employer Type: Public Company
Ticker Symbol: ACAS (NASDAQ)
Revenue: $336.1 million (FYE 12/04)
Net Income: $281.4 million
No. of Employees: 229
No. of Offices: 9

KEY COMPETITORS

Allied Capital
CapitalSource
Gladstone Capital

EMPLOYMENT CONTACT

Lionel Ferguson
Senior Vice President
Human Resources
Fax: (301) 654-6714
E-mail:
Lionel.Ferguson@AmericanCapital.com

THE SCOOP

Bigger is better

Since its initial public offering in 1997, American Capital has grown to become the world's largest business development company (a BDC is a public buyout firm). For the past two years, the publicly traded buyout and mezzanine fund has been the No. 1 investor in middle-market companies, with a market share of around 5 to 6 percent. Reflecting its new position at the top, the firm also boasts the largest team in the industry, with more than 200 professionals working out of nine offices in the U.S. and Europe. American Capital's staff has nearly quadrupled since 2000, and the firm now has twice as many principals as it did three years ago. Another sign of growth, in 2004, the private equity group increased its new investments five fold, for a record of approximately $2 billion in some 42 new portfolio companies.

The year 2005 is already scheduled to be another record-breaking one; as of October, the firm had already invested $2.2 billion, and in the second quarter of 2005 alone, American Capital closed $903 million in new investments. During that same quarter, the firm reported revenue of $131.7 million, up 125 percent from the second quarter of 2004. The firm's positive financial results earned praise from *BusinessWeek* in July 2005. American Capital made the magazine's list of "double-barrel growth" companies. To make the list, companies had to demonstrate consistent sales growth for the past five years, year-over-year quarterly sales growth of more than 25 percent and net margins of over 25 percent.

Three's company

American Capital has three main lines of business. It is a financial partner in management and employee buyouts; provides senior debt, mezzanine and equity financing for buyouts led by private equity firms; and provides capital directly to private and small public companies. To date, American Capital has invested more than $5 billion in over 170 portfolio companies in industries ranging from construction and transportation to consumer and food products. The company invests up to $250 million, with an average investment of around $28 million. Recent deals for American Capital include the $117 million investment in Bushnell Performance Optics in August 2005; the $111 million buyout of Fosbel Holdings, a global services and repair company, also in August; the $188 million investment in the buyout of the Potpourri Group in June 2005; and the $108 million investment in the buyout of FutureLogic, an embedded thermal printing solutions company, in February 2005.

Up next: Europe

American Capital is in the process of setting up its European affiliate, European Capital. The European branch will work out of offices in London and Paris and will perform the same functions as the American arm. Natalie Faure Beaulieu heads up the firm's London outpost; Jean Eichenlaub is the managing director in Paris.

GETTING HIRED

Candidates interested in working for American Capital should contact Lionel Ferguson, the senior vice president of human resources. He can be reached via fax at (301) 654-6714 or e-mail at Lionel.Ferguson@AmericanCapital.com.

Apax Partners, Inc.

445 Park Avenue, 11th Floor
New York, NY 10022
Phone: (212) 753-6300
Fax: (212) 319-6155
www.apax.com

THE STATS

CEO: Martin Halusa
Employer Type: Private Company
No. of Employees: 140
No. of Offices: 11

KEY COMPETITORS

Draper Fisher Jurvetson
Hummer Winblad
Kleiner Perkins

EMPLOYMENT CONTACT

E-mail: careers@apax.com

Visit Vault at **www.vault.com** for insider company profiles, expert advice,
career message boards, expert resume reviews, the Vault Job Board and more.

VAULT CAREER LIBRARY   15

THE SCOOP

Still kicking

Apax Partners is a veteran in the private equity biz, tracing its roots back to 1969 when the investment firm was known as Alan Patricof Associates. But this old-timer still knows how to move and shake, completing a bevy of new deals in the past year. In 2005, the private equity group acquired Spanish food group Grupo Panrico, foreign exchange specialist Travelex, home-decoration retail chains Heytens and Mondial Tissues and Israeli telecom company Bezeq - to name a few. And in February 2005, Apax Partners expanded its U.S. buyout presence through a merger with Saunders Karp & Megrue (SKM). To date, the company has raised more than $20 billion and invested in some 340 companies.

Global powerhouse

If you ask John Megrue, co-CEO of Apax Partners' U.S. operations, the private equity industry is undergoing a polarization of sorts. On the one hand, there are firms that want to become global leaders; on the other, there are those that want to become niche specialists. Apax Partners, says Megrue, wants to be in the first group. With 11 offices in the U.S., Israel, Europe and, most recently, Hong Kong, and a strong history to build on, the private equity group is well-positioned. While the U.S. arm typically invests in middle-market buyouts (in the range of $100 million to $1 billion), the firm's European-Israeli operations usually goes for cross-border, billion-plus-dollar transactions. As a whole, Apax targets deals in five sectors: tech and telecom, consumer and retail, media, health care, and financial services.

The times they are a-changin'

Although many private equity firms have struggled with the transition from one generation to the next, Apax Partners is an exception. Sir Ronald and other partners were already discussing succession back in the late 1990s, ultimately agreeing to a retirement age ceiling of 60. So in January 2004, less than two years from his 60th birthday, co-founder Sir Ronald Cohen stepped down as chief executive, naming Martin Halusa as his successor. Sir Ronald stayed on as chairman, maintaining a leadership position but giving Halusa significant breathing room, and retired from that office in August 2005. While some wonder how the firm will fare with Sir Ronald gone, Halusa isn't exactly a newbie; he's been with Apax Partners for 15 years and describes the management changes at Apax as "organic, rather than revolutionary."

The private equity group's merger with SKM is another sign of changing times. In the past, the firm's U.S. division has been focused on smaller venture-capital style investing – think first- and second-stage and mezzanine financing to high-tech, retail and communications companies such as America Online, Apple Computer and Office Depot. The combination with Connecticut-based SKM will allow Apax to handle bigger buyout deals in the U.S. Still, the firm isn't forgoing the venture business, even though the dual focus (venture capital and buyouts) is atypical. In June 2005, Halusa told *Real Deals*, "You have to be at the venture capital stages to be able to do a large deal because that is where a lot of the industry knowledge comes from."

Looking East

As of yet, Apax Partners doesn't have a buyout operation in Asia, but the private equity firm is putting all the pieces in place. In mid-2005, the company opened an office in Hong Kong, headed up by senior partner Max Burger-Calderon. For the time being, the outpost is involved in finding suppliers, manufacturers and distribution outlets for portfolio companies.

GETTING HIRED

Candidates interested in joining the Apax team should send a resume and cover letter to careers@apax.com

Visit Vault at **www.vault.com** for insider company profiles, expert advice, career message boards, expert resume reviews, the Vault Job Board and more.

VAULT CAREER LIBRARY   17

Bain Capital

111 Huntington Avenue
Boston, MA 02199
Phone: (617) 516-2000
Fax: (617) 516-2010
www.baincapital.com

THE STATS

Managing Director: Joshua Bekenstein
Employer Type: Private Company
No. of Employees: 175
No. of Offices: 4

KEY COMPETITORS

Summit Partners
Texas Pacific Group
Thomas H. Lee Partners

EMPLOYMENT CONTACT

See "careers" at
www.baincapital.com

THE SCOOP

Dealmaker

Bain Capital traces its roots back to 1984, when Bain & Company partners Mitt Romney (the current Governor of Massachusetts), T. Coleman Andrews and Eric Kriss decided to leverage their private equity know-how by forming their own leveraged buyout and venture capital firm. Today, the Boston-based private equity firm has invested in more than 225 companies and has some $25 billion in assets under management. Notable deals in 2005 include the $4.3 billion buyout of all 30 teams in the National Hockey League, the $3.1 billion acquisition of Warner Chilcott and the $6.6 billion purchase of Toys R Us. Bain was also part of a consortium of private equity firms led by Silver Lake Partners to acquire SunGard Data Systems. The deal, completed in August 2005, was valued at $11.4 billion, making it the largest technology privatization and the second largest leveraged buyout ever completed.

The one, the many

Bain Capital has offices in Boston, New York, London and Munich, and employs more than 175 deal professionals. Although the majority of Bain's efforts are geared toward private equity (through Bain Capital Private Equity and its European affiliate Bain Capital Limited), the company also dabbles in venture capital, public equity and leverage debt assets. Absolute Return Capital (ARC) manages $600 million of capital in fixed income, equity and commodity markets; Bain Capital Ventures, the venture capital arm, focuses on seed through late-growth equity investments in technology companies; Brookside Capital is Bain's public equity affiliate, targeting publicly traded companies with long-term growth potential; and Sankaty Advisors invests in high-yield securities.

Value-added

With its close ties to Bain & Company, it should come as no surprise that Bain Capital's investment approach draws on its partners' consulting expertise. According to the firm, its investment professionals evaluate companies on a "people-intensive, consulting-based due diligence process" that looks at "financial performance, market potential, industry attractiveness and competitive position." Once Bain invests in a company, it takes an active role in improving the business.

Visit Vault at **www.vault.com** for insider company profiles, expert advice, career message boards, expert resume reviews, the Vault Job Board and more.

VAULT CAREER LIBRARY   19

Hollywood ending?

These days, moviegoers are something of a dying breed. According to media information company Nielsen Entertainment, as of September 2005, box office sales were down about 7 percent for the year. The question many people are asking themselves is, "Do I want to see the movie in the theater or should I wait for the DVD?" With movies being released on DVD much faster now than in the past, an increasing number of viewers are choosing to wait it out to save several bucks. A recent Associated Press-AOL poll revealed that nearly three-fourths of Americans would rather rent. In July 2005, in a move geared toward survival, AMC agreed to acquire Loews Cineplex Entertainment Corp, both of which had been acquired last year by a group of private investors. Bain Capital, together with the Carlyle Group and Spectrum Equity Investors, bought Loews for $1.5 billion; following the merger, the private-equity owners will own 40 percent of the combined company. Bain Capital, like the rest of the parties involved, is most likely hoping for a Hollywood ending. Other media investments for the private equity group include Artisan Entertainment and GoCom Communications.

GETTING HIRED

Unlike many private equity groups, Bain Capital has both a web site and a career page ("careers" at www.baincapital.com). Candidates interested in working for the buyout firm, can learn more about current job openings – and apply – online. For example, the company offers a two-year associate program in any of its four offices, which starts off with a multi-week training program designed to introduce newcomers to Bain's "value-added" investment approach. Interested individuals are encouraged to apply immediately for the Summer/Fall of 2006.

The Blackstone Group

345 Park Avenue
New York, NY 10154
Phone: (212) 583-5000
Fax: (212) 583-5712
www.blackstone.com

THE STATS

Chairman & CEO: Stephen A.
Schwarzman
Employer Type: Private Company
No. of Employees: 500+
No. of Offices: 8

Visit Vault at **www.vault.com** for insider company profiles, expert advice,
career message boards, expert resume reviews, the Vault Job Board and more.

VAULT CAREER LIBRARY

21

THE SCOOP

B is for big

The Blackstone Group got its start in 1985 as an M&A advisory boutique with a staff of four and a balance sheet of $400,000. Today, the group boasts expertise in a number of areas – including corporate debt, real estate, asset management and advisory services – but its private equity business has become its bread and butter. Blackstone's first buyout fund closed in 1987 at $950 million, making it the largest first-time fund ever. Fifteen years later, Blackstone set another record when it established its $6.45 billion Blackstone Capital Partners IV fund.

In total, the firm has raised more than $14 billion across five private equity funds, and as Blackstone's funds get larger, so do its deals. The Blackstone-led buyout of TRW Automotive, completed in March 2003, was the largest LBO since RJR Nabisco in 1988.

And in September 2003, Blackstone teamed up with Goldman Sachs and Apollo Management to acquire Ondeo Nalco, the world's leading provider of water-treatment services, for $4.2 billion. More recently, in August 2005, Blackstone was involved in another record-breaking deal, the $11.3 billion acquisition of SunGard Data Systems. In total, Blackstone has invested in over 87 companies worth more than $110 billion.

B-list industry investing

Blackstone invests in what it calls "out of favor" industries. Ignoring swings in conventional wisdom about the attractiveness of certain sectors, Blackstone puts its money in "B-list" industries such as cable television, rural cellular, refining and automotive parts. The company's investment approach also includes partnerships with leading corporations, such as AOL Time Warner, AT&T and Sony, rigorous due diligence and an active role in monitoring portfolio companies. The firm has a dedicated senior operating partner who is responsible for overseeing the strategic, operational and financial performance of its investments, and employs former C-level executives who act as advisors and board members.

Building blocks

In July 2005, Blackstone completed the acquisition of Merlin Entertainment, an operator of branded visitor attractions under the Sea Life, Dungeons, Seal Sanctuary and Earth Explorer brands for £102.5 million. The transaction indicates the firm's seriousness about the leisure sector and, more specifically, European attractions and theme parks. Sources say the private equity group will use the deal as a building block to acquire the Legoland portfolio, for which Blackstone is competing with Dubai International.

Another sector of interest to Blackstone is energy. In October 2005, the private equity group acquired an 80 percent stake in Sithe Global Power. Together with Reservoir Capital Group, which owns the remaining 20 percent interest, Blackstone plans to invest more than $500 million of equity in the company's power plant projects. Previous energy investments include Premcor, Inc., a U.S. refiner of petroleum products (acquired by Valero in 2005); Texas Genco, a Houston-based wholesale electric power generating company; Foundation Coal, a U.S. coal mining company; and Kosmos Energy, an oil exploration company.

Going global

While Blackstone's primary market is North America, the New York-based firm has increased its focus on Europe and Asia in recent years. The group opened an office in London in August 2000, an outpost in Hamburg in September 2003 and an office in Mumbai in May 2005. The group also entered into a strategic alliance with Roland Berger Strategy Consultants GmbH, one of Europe's top management consultancy, in February 2001. The partnership gives Blackstone access to intellectual capital and local knowledge of key European markets.

Healthy choice

With an eye on the pharmaceuticals and health care markets, in April 2003, Blackstone teamed up with Lodewijk de Vink, former chairman, president and CEO of Warner-Lambert; Aleksander Erdeljan, former CEO and Chairman of RP Scherer; and Doug Rogers, a former member of Donaldson, Lufkin & Jenrette's health care merchant banking group. Theses individuals make up Blackstone Health Care Partners and are charged with sourcing, analyzing and overseeing investments for the private equity group in the health care arena.

More than just private equity

Although Blackstone's private equity group has earned the firm an elite status, its other divisions should not be discounted. The firm's M&A group, for example, has had its hands in several high-profile transactions over the years, including two big financial services deals. In 2000, Blackstone advised PaineWebber on its $10.8 billion sale to UBS, and Alliance Capital Management on its $3.5 billion purchase of Sanford C. Bernstein. More recently, in early 2005, the firm advised Comcast on its $18 billion acquisition of Adelphia Communications.

Blackstone's restructuring department has advised companies and creditors in more than 150 situations, involving $315 billion of total liabilities. In an attempt to cut costs to avoid bankruptcy, Delta Air Lines hired Blackstone to assist with its restructuring efforts. RCN Corporation recently switched from Merrill Lynch to Blackstone for its financial restructuring negotiations with its senior secured lenders. Blackstone also acted as lead advisor in the restructurings of both Enron and Global Crossing.

The real estate group, operating out of the New York, London and Paris offices, boasts that it owns more than 13 million square feet of real estate in Boston, New York, San Francisco and Washington, D.C. All told, the unit may have the largest real estate portfolio on the Street. In 2004, the group made a number of key acquisitions, including Extended Stay America for $3.2 billion, Prime Hospitality Corp. for $790 million, and Boca Resorts for $1.2 billion. More recently, in August 2005, Blackstone's real estate division snatched up the luxury hotel group Wyndham International for $1.4 billion.

Blackstone's corporate debt group is actually two businesses: Blackstone Mezzanine Advisors and Blackstone Debt Advisors (BDA). Blackstone's mezzanine fund of $1.1 billion is one of the largest of its kind and has investments in firms such as 24 Hour Fitness Worldwide and Vitamin Shoppe Industries. BDA is a relatively new group (created in 2002) and has more than $3 billion of CDO (Collateralized Debt Obligation) funds for investment predominantly in senior secured loans. Last but definitely not least is the Blackstone Alternative Asset Management unit (headed by BAAM president and CEO J. Tomilson Hill), which has almost $9 billion of assets under management in funds of hedge funds.

GETTING HIRED

To learn more about job opportunities with Blackstone, check out the careers section of the company web site. There, the firm provides information on campus recruiting, as well as experienced and international hiring. The group hires recent undergraduates as analysts and recent MBAs as associates. Recruiting typically takes place in the fall for full-time programs and in January for internships. Schools on Blackstone's campus schedule include Harvard, University of Michigan, University of Pennsylvania, University of Texas at Austin and UVA. Students whose school Blackstone does not visit can apply for these programs online. The recruiting process typically involves an on-campus interview followed by one or two rounds at the firm's New York office.

Experienced hires can contact the firm via an online application. International hires should contact the London Human Resources department at recruitingeurope@blackstone.com. Blackstone's private equity group operates in London, Hamburg and Mumbai.

The Carlyle Group

1001 Pennsylvania Avenue, NW
Washington, D.C. 20004-2505
Phone: (202) 729-5626
Fax: (202) 347-1818
www.thecarlylegroup.com

THE STATS

Chairman: Louis V. Gerstner Jr.
Employer Type: Private Company
No. of Employees: 600+
No. of Offices: 24

KEY COMPETITORS

Hicks Muse
KKR
Texas Pacific Group

EMPLOYMENT CONTACT

United States: hrusa@carlyle.com
Europe: hreurope@carlyle.com
Asia: hrasia@carlyle.com
Japan: hrjapan@carlyle.com

THE SCOOP

Carlyle talks baseball

With nearly $31 billion under management, the Carlyle Group is one of the world's largest private equity firms. Since the firm's founding in 1987, the group has invested $14.3 billion in 414 transactions. But the Washington, D.C.-based company is quick to tell you that it doesn't "swing for the fences" – or go for home-runs. Instead, the group pursues a conservative investment approach, preferring to hit more singles (and doubles and triples) with fewer strikeouts. Indeed, Carlyle points to its caution as a trait that sets it apart from competitors – that and its team of more than 300 investment professionals, including 138 MBAs, 24 JDs and 14 MD/PhDs.

Although the group considers investments in a wide range of industries, it focuses on a few key sectors, including telecom and media, real estate, aerospace, information technology, energy and industrial. Although the firm dabbles in venture capital, leveraged finance and real-estate, the majority of its deals are management-led buyouts. Geographically, the Carlyle Group is a global company with 24 offices in 13 countries, and its European and Asian investments account for nearly 30 percent of assets.

Asian invasion

In March 2005, the Carlyle Group announced a significant expansion of its pan-Asian investment activities, with the planned opening of new offices in Beijing, Mumbai and Sydney. As of September 2005, all three outposts were up and running. In total, the Carlyle Asia buyout group has six managing directors and 14 additional investment professionals working out of eight offices.

The private equity group first got involved in Asia in 1998 when the firm acquired a controlling stake in Korea's KorAm Bank for $450 million. In April 2004, KorAm was sold to Citigroup for $2.7 billion, representing a $650 million profit for Carlyle and a 250 percent return on investment for the group's investors. So what is the group's recipe for success? Combine a new CEO and management team with streamlined operations, wait three to five years, then sell.

Recent investments include a $400 million investment in Shanghai's China Pacific Life Insurance Co. and a 60 percent stake in the $2.1 billion takeover of Japanese cell-phone maker DDI Pocket (recently renamed Willcom Inc.). As of February 2005, the company had invested $4 billion in the region, with a $750 million fund

Visit Vault at **www.vault.com** for insider company profiles, expert advice, career message boards, expert resume reviews, the Vault Job Board and more.

VAULT CAREER LIBRARY   27

focused on Korea, China and Taiwan, and plans to raise a $1.25 to $1.5 billion fund for further investments.

Satellites and automobiles

The Carlyle Group has also been busy outside of Asia Pacific. In September 2005, for example, the private equity group joined forces with Clayton, Dubilier & Rice and Merrill Lynch Global Private Equity to acquire Hertz, the world's largest vehicle rental group, from Ford Motor Company for $15 billion – beating out other private equity groups vying for the investment.

Just a month earlier, in August 2005, the firm exited an investment in satellite operator PanAmSat, which was sold to competitor Intelsat. Back in 2004, the Carlyle Group, together with Kohlberg, Kravis Roberts (KKR) and Providence Equity Partners, acquired PanAmSat for $2.6 billion. The $3.2 billion price tag paid by Intelsat represents a $600 million gain for the private equity consortium. What's more, the investors had already made millions off the investment by taking 42 percent of PanAmSat public in an IPO that raised $2.9 billion.

GETTING HIRED

The Carlyle Group offers opportunities for investment professionals, support professionals, associates and senior associates. Investment professionals are involved in the analysis, execution, monitoring and exit of private equity investments. Support professionals are part of the investor services team, which encompasses accounting, administration, corporate communications, human resources, information technology, investor relations and legal. Associates are typically recent undergraduates with a strong GPA and two years of investment banking or consulting experience. Associates at the Carlyle Group go through a formal two-year program. Senior associates generally hold an MBA and have three to four years of private equity, investment banking or consulting experience. Candidates interested in applying for a position at the Carlyle Group should send a resume and cover letter to the appropriate region (U.S., Europe, Asia or Japan).

Cerberus Capital Management

299 Park Avenue
New York, NY 10171
Phone: (212) 891-2100
Fax: (212) 891-1540

THE STATS

Senior Managing Director: Stephen
A. Feinberg
Employer Type: Private Company

KEY COMPETITORS

Blackstone Group
KKR
Texas Pacific Group

EMPLOYMENT CONTACT

Phone: (212) 891-2100

Visit Vault at **www.vault.com** for insider company profiles, expert advice,
career message boards, expert resume reviews, the Vault Job Board and more.

VAULT CAREER LIBRARY   29

THE SCOOP

The man behind the dog

Although Cerberus Capital Management is named after the three-headed dog that guards the gates of hell in Greek mythology, the investment company is not as ferocious as its name implies. The group never makes hostile bids, preferring to work with willing partners to grow target companies. Founded in 1992, Cerberus is headed up by Stephen A. Feinberg, a Princeton graduate who got his start at Drexel Burnham Lambert (the notorious investment bank that was dissolved in 1990 due to securities fraud). But Feinberg, like Cerberus, is not necessarily what he seems at first glance. The son of a steel salesman, Feinberg still thinks of himself as "blue collar" (even though he earned around $50 million in 2004), and friends say he drives a Ford pickup truck, drinks Budweiser, and enjoys hunting pheasants and partridges. He is also intensely private, perhaps one of the reasons why Cerberus doesn't have a web site.

Defying definition

To some extent, Cerberus Capital Management defies definition. It is neither a traditional hedge fund nor your average buyout firm. The company's 12 funds are a hodgepodge of loans, real estate, debt and other investments, and have timeframes that range from six months to 12 years. Sources say Feinberg hopes to run his business more like a Fortune 500 corporation than a trading operation. Cerberus calls on 80 seasoned executives – including Timothy F. Price, the former president of MCI Communications and George E. Hamilton, a past executive at Newell Rubbermaid – to come up with investment ideas, perform due diligence and run the companies it acquires. While other investment firms employ former CEOs, Cerberus has more of them, and its executives play a much more active role. Another unique aspect of Feinberg's company is his approach to financing. In 1996, the senior managing director started Cerberus' own finance company, and in 2003, the firm acquired Japan's Aozora Bank, which Feinberg uses to lend money to portfolio companies.

Watch out for this watchdog

One thing's certain, with $16 billion in assets under management, Cerberus is a force to be reckoned with. In the past decade, the firm has snatched up 28 companies and acquired stakes in another 15. The company has its claws (or, perhaps more appropriately, paws) in companies like Burger King, the National and Alamo car-rental chains and Warner Hollywood Studios. Cerberus also has its watchful eyes on Boise, Id. food chain Albertson's, which is expected to go for around $16 billion, potentially the largest deal since KKR purchased RJR Nabisco for $31 billion in 1989; Morgan Stanley's aircraft-leasing business, worth up to $2 billion; and Israel's second largest bank, Bank Leumi. The company's success stories include software company SSA Global, whose stock has shot up 41 percent since its May 2005 IPO; Vanguard Car Rental USA, parent to National and Alamo, which is expected to go public for around $2 billion (Feinberg bought the pair for $400 million); and communications-services provider Teleglobe International Holdings, on which Cerberus doubled its money when it sold off a 66 percent stake in the firm in July 2005.

Cerberus has had a few flops along the way. BlueLinx Holdings Inc., a building-material wholesale company that Cerberus took public in December 2004, hasn't performed well despite boom times for the housing market. More devastating for Cerberus is the fact that bottle maker Anchor Glass Container filed for bankruptcy in August 2005, and Anchor shareholders have filed a class action suit against Cerberus, alleging the firm hid information about a lost contract before Anchor's IPO in 2003.

The softer side

The Cerberus name doesn't always sit well with prospective investments. Last year, for example, the firm almost lost out on a deal with ACE Aviation Holdings (parent company to Air Canada) because the Canadian company feared Cerberus might tear the airline apart. Feinberg clung onto the deal only after he assured ACE that Cerberus wouldn't sell its 9 percent stake for at least two years. The addition of former U.S. Vice President Dan Quayle has helped soften Cerberus' image to some extent. Quayle came on board in 2000 after dropping out of the Presidential race and now serves as chairman of the Cerberus advisory board. Quayle uses his connections to scout out deals in North America, Europe and Asia, and helped the firm open an office in Germany in 2003.

Rumor mill

A *Women's Wear Daily* story in March 2005 reported that Cerberus may be contemplating J.C. Penney as its next target. Yet another article, in July 2005, speculated that the investment firm has its eye of the Northern Department Store Group of Saks, Inc. Such rumors are certainly not far flung, as Cerberus has a history of investing in retailers. Past acquisitions include the 257-store Mervyn's chain

Visit Vault at **www.vault.com** for insider company profiles, expert advice, career message boards, expert resume reviews, the Vault Job Board and more.

VAULT CAREER LIBRARY   31

(from Target), sport brand Fila and Rafaella Sportswear. What's more, former Penney executive Vanessa Castagna is now an employee of Cerberus. Still, insiders say Cerberus won't buy Penney (word is still out on Saks) because the company doesn't fit the firm's distressed company profile – Penney rebounded from a $928 million net loss in 2003 to a $524 million net gain.

GETTING HIRED

New York-based Cerberus has offices in Chicago, Los Angeles, Japan, Korea, Taiwan and Germany. Perhaps because of Feinberg's penchant for privacy, the investment firm does not have a web site. Individuals interested in working for Cerberus should contact the firm's headquarters directly.

Charterhouse Group, Inc.

535 Madison Avenue, 28th Floor
New York, NY 10022-4299
Phone: (212) 584-3200
Fax: (212) 750-9704
www.charterhousegroup.com

THE STATS

Chairman: Merril M. Halpern
Employer Type: Private Company
No. of Employees: 20
No. of Offices: 1

EMPLOYMENT CONTACT

employment@charterhousegroup.com

THE SCOOP

Middle of the road

The Charterhouse Group was founded in 1973 by Merril Halpern, now chairman of the investment firm. Charterhouse focuses on middle-market companies in the business services, health care services and consumer industries; its portfolio includes companies such as American Disposal Services (waste management), Charter Communications (cable television), Insignia Financial Group (real estate asset management), Cross Country Healthcare (health care staffing), Del Monte Foods and Dreyer's Grand Ice Cream. The firm currently manages over $1.3 billion in capital and has invested over $1.4 billion in more than 80 businesses. Charterhouse is based in New York and employs around 20 investment professionals.

Investment formula

Charterhouse has a fairly specific formula when it comes to making investments. The group seeks out companies with an enterprise values in the range of $100 million to $500 million, a strong management team, a leading industry position, competitive advantages – such as brand recognition and proprietary products, processes or customer relationships – and a scalable business model. The firm also looks for the opportunity to invest at least $30 million over the life of the investment and the ability to exert board influence.

Healthy living

Charterhouse recently purchased Amerifit Nutrition, a marketer of nutritional supplements and wellness products, and the Vermont Bread Company, a maker of natural and organic bread, muffins and bakery items. Both companies, acquired in April 2005, have already made acquisitions of their own under the direction of the Charterhouse Group. In July 2005, Vermont Bread snatched up the Adams Bakery Corporation, maker of The Baker brand of breads, rolls, granola and other baked goods; in August 2005, Vermont Bread and Adams Bakery merged with Rudi's Organic Bakery. Together, the baking companies are known as the Charter Baking Company. In October 2005, Amerifit bought the women's health products division of Polymedica Corporation for $45 million.

GETTING HIRED

The firm does not have a career web site or information about positions or the hiring process. Interested candidates should contact the firm via e-mail at employment@charterhousegroup.com.

Visit Vault at **www.vault.com** for insider company profiles, expert advice,
career message boards, expert resume reviews, the Vault Job Board and more.

V/\ULT CAREER LIBRARY   35

Clayton, Dubilier & Rice

375 Park Avenue, 18th Floor
New York, NY 10152
Phone: (212) 407-5200
Fax: (212) 407-5252
www.cdr-inc.com

THE STATS

President & CEO: Donald J. Gogel
Employer Type: Private Company
No. of Employees: 29
No. of Offices: 2

KEY COMPETITORS

Hicks Muse
KKR
Texas Pacific Group

EMPLOYMENT CONTACT

Phone: (212) 407-5200

THE SCOOP

Rulers of restoration

Founded in 1978, Clayton, Dubilier & Rice (CD&R) is one of the oldest and most respected firms in the private equity business. The New York-based firm has made a name for itself by honing in on non-core divisions of large corporations and other underachieving businesses – and turning them around. Take Lexmark International, for example, IBM's former typewriter division. CD&R acquired the business unit from IBM in 1991 and transformed it from a typewriter manufacturer into a laser and inkjet printer company. Kinko's is another success story. When the private equity group invested in Kinko's back in 1996, the company had the best brand name in the business, but was experiencing major growing pains. CD&R installed new management and invested in new technology to restructure Kinko's into a single, centralized corporation and increase profitability. In February 2004, FedEx Corporation doled out $2.4 billion for the new and improved Kinko's.

The firm's latest project is the Hertz Corporation. In September 2005, the private equity group joined forces with the Carlyle Group and Merrill Lynch Private Equity to acquire the Hertz Corporation from Ford Motor Company for approximately $15 billion. CD&R partner George W. Tamke will serve as chairman of the board of directors. To date, CD&R has invested more than $5.5 billion in 37 deals. The firm is currently managing its sixth fund, which has committed capital of $3.5 billion.

Europe, land of opportunity

In 2004, private equity groups invested $156 billion in European companies, up 66 percent from 2000. Europe, it seems, is the new hot spot for private equity – and CD&R is certainly a major player. The firm's $4.5 billion buyout of French electrical equipment supplier Rexel was the largest European public to private transaction ever. The deal, which was completed in March 2005, was also the third largest private equity buyout in Europe to date. Other international transactions for Clayton, Dubilier & Rice include VWR International, a global distributor of scientific supplies, in April 2004, and Culligan, a global provider of water treatment products and services, in September 2004. For the most part, CD&R invests in companies in the U.K., Italy and Germany, but says it is currently evaluating the markets in France and other European countries.

Hands-on

All in, Clayton Dubilier & Rice has 29 professionals working out of offices in New York and London. While they may not be numerous, the firm's partners boast a wealth of experience and many of them are former chief-level executives. Ex-GE CEO Jack Welch, for example, came on board as special partner back in 2001. At the time, president and CEO Daniel Gogel (then chairman) told *BusinessWeek* that he wasn't sure exactly what Jack would do, but he was happy to enjoy the "halo effect" of having him on board. For the most part, former executives like Welch are involved in hands-on management, helping companies stimulate sales growth, change the path to market, shorten product development cycles, improve manufacturing productivity, manage working capital, reduce costs and establish results-driven incentive plans.

GETTING HIRED

Clayton, Dubilier & Rice does not provide career information on its web site. Individuals interested in working for the private equity group should contact the firm directly at its headquarters in New York.

CSFB Private Equity

11 Madison Avenue
New York, NY 10010
Phone: (212) 325-2000
www.csfb.com

DEPARTMENTS

Customized Fund Investment Group
Equity Funds
Mezzanine Funds
Real Estate
Secondary Funds
Sprout Group

THE STATS

**President, CSFB & Head of
Alternative Capital:** Brian D. Finn
Employer Type: Unit of Credit Suisse
Group
No. of Employees: 150
No. of Offices: 7

KEY COMPETITORS

Hicks Muse
KKR
Texas Pacific Group

EMPLOYMENT CONTACT

Visit the "career opportunities"
section site of www.csfb.com

Visit Vault at **www.vault.com** for insider company profiles, expert advice,
career message boards, expert resume reviews, the Vault Job Board and more.

V/\ULT CAREER LIBRARY   39

THE SCOOP

Swiss investing

CSFB Private Equity is a unit of Swiss banking behemoth Credit Suisse Group. And the unit is a somewhat of a behemoth itself. The private equity arm, which specifically falls under Credit Suisse's alternative capital division, has more than $25 billion in funds under management. It focuses on domestic and international leveraged buyouts, structured equity investments, mezzanine investments, real estate investments, venture capital and growth capital investments, and investments in other private equity funds. The unit also comprises investment firms DLJ Merchant Banking Partners, which acts as a lead principal investor in middle market companies and focuses on deals where it can invest up to $200 million in equity, and the Sprout Group, which invests private equity in growth companies. Major CSFB Private Equity holdings include Germany-based bathroom fixture maker Grohe Water Technology and U.S.-based technology firm Egenera.

In the U.S., CSFB Private Equity has offices in New York, Houston, Los Angeles, and Menlo Park, Calif. Abroad, the unit has offices in London, Buenos Aires and Tokyo. It has more than 150 investment professionals and, to date, has completed more than 800 transactions worth over $120 billion in total transaction value.

At the top of the org chart

The unit's ultimate parent, Credit Suisse Group, is a leading global financial services company headquartered in Zurich. Along with its investment banking division, which serves global institutional, corporate, government and individual clients in its role as a financial intermediary, Credit Suisse also services private clients, small and medium-sized companies with private banking products, and offers financial advisory services and asset management. Through its Winterthur operation, Credit Suisse provides pension and insurance solutions.

Credit Suisse Group's registered shares (CSGN) are listed in Switzerland and in the form of American Depositary Shares (CSR) in New York. Credit Suisse employs approximately 60,000 people worldwide. Beginning in January 2006, Credit Suisse's three main divisions – Corporate & Investment Banking, Private Banking and Asset Management – will operate under one brand name, "Credit Suisse." Previously, in December 2004, Credit Suisse Group announced that it would integrate its Corporate & Investment Banking division (the former CSFB) into the parent company over the next two years in an effort to create a "more focused franchise." Credit Suisse Group's chief executive, Oswald J. Grubel, said he wanted to create "one bank" by streamlining Credit Suisse and CSFB into three business lines: private clients, corporate and investment banking clients, and asset management (under which falls alternative capital and, under that, CSFB Private Equity).

As part of its "one bank" strategy, Credit Suisse believes it should be united behind one brand. According to Credit Suisse, extensive internal and external research supported and reinforced their decision. The new unified expression of its brand, including a new logo, will be put in place on January 1, 2006, at which time the CSFB brand will be retired and "Credit Suisse" will be the one brand going forward, which will likely mean a name change for CSFB Private Equity.

Dealings

In May 2004, CSFB Private Equity, along with Mid Ocean Partners, acquired Washington, D.C.-based Thompson Publishing Group. A month earlier, in April, CSFB Private Equity and KKR put up equity to help Princeton, N.J.-based Rockwood Specialties Group acquire four businesses from Germany-based Dynamit Nobel, Troisdorf to form a new specialty chemicals group with combined revenue of $2.5 billion. The deal created one of the world's largest specialty chemical companies. More recently, in September 2005, a consortium of private equity firms, including GS Capital Partners, the Blackstone Group and CSFB Private Equity's DLJ Merchant Banking, announced its intention to acquire Texas-based insurer UICI, committing to invest over $1 billion of equity in the transaction.

GETTING HIRED

Interested candidates should check out the "career opportunities" site of www.csfb.com to find information about private equity jobs at Credit Suisse. The site provides a list of upcoming on-campus recruiting events, links to online applications, descriptions of specific business units, and interviewing tips and descriptions of duties from insiders, among other hiring information.

In its alternative capital division, the firm offers a range of full-time programs for analysts – typically undergrads. According to the firm, "As a first-year analyst, you receive intensive classroom training for eight weeks in New York, as part of our firm-wide training program. Components of this training will include: an orientation to the firm, basics of accounting, corporate finance, financial modeling, training on the

Visit Vault at **www.vault.com** for insider company profiles, expert advice, career message boards, expert resume reviews, the Vault Job Board and more.

VAULT CAREER LIBRARY

41

firm's technology systems and database capabilities." Undergrads interested in CSFB Private Equity positions typically join DLJ Partners as mezzanine fund analysts. Duties include "analyzing investment opportunities, preparing financial model, conducting operational and financial due diligence, drafting investment committee memoranda, monitoring portfolio company performance, and preparing limited partner presentation and fundraising materials."

Graduate students typically join CSFB Private Equity as merchant banking associates. According to the firm, applicants "must have prior investment banking and/or private equity experience, be in their final year of a graduate degree program and be highly motivated, creative individuals who have demonstrated academic achievement, specifically in finance, marketing and accounting."

Evercore Partners

55 East 52nd Street, 43rd Floor
New York, NY 10055
Phone: (212) 857-3100
Fax: (212) 857-3101
www.evercore.com

THE STATS

Chairman & Co-CEO: Roger C. Altman
Co-CEO: Austin M. Beutner
Employer Type: Private Company
Revenue: $110 million (est.)
No. of Employees: 100
No. of Offices: 3

EMPLOYMENT CONTACT

Analyst recruiting:
analystrecruiting@evercore.com
Experienced hires:
recruiting@evercore.com

THE SCOOP

Core info

Part investor, part advisor, Evercore Partners was founded in 1996 by Blackstone alumni Roger Altman and Austin Beutner (now the firm's co-CEOs). The firm manages over $1.2 billion, funded by prominent U.S. and international investors, through its private equity and venture capital divisions, Evercore Capital Partners and Evercore Ventures, respectively. Its portfolio companies include American Media (publisher of *National Enquirer* and *Star* magazines), Michigan Electric Transmission and advertising firm Vertis. Most recently, in April 2005, Evercore invested $84 million in a 70 percent stake in Diagnostic Imaging Group, a supplier of scheduling, billing and accounting services to operators of radiology imaging clinics. Evercore also provides financial advisory and restructuring advisory to major corporations and their interest holders.

Private information

Evercore Capital Partners generally targets companies with an enterprise value of at least $100 million, although it has completed a handful of transactions valued at over $4 billion in partnership with other investors. The private equity group devotes considerable time and resources to its investments; Evercore's investment professionals work with portfolio companies to determine business strategy, allocate capital and evaluate expansion and acquisition opportunities (the firm's expertise in advisory services comes in handy).

Throughout the investment process, the private equity arm calls on a team of advisors to originate investments, evaluate investments and add value once an investment has been made. The advisory board includes high-profile individuals such as Roger A. Enrico, the former chairman and CEO of PepsiCo, and W. Michael Blumenthal, the former chairman and CEO of both Unisys Corporation and Bendix Corporation, as well as the former U.S. Treasury Secretary. Evercore's team of private equity investment professionals is also an impressive bunch. John Dillon, for example, the private equity group's vice chairman, served as chairman and CEO of International Paper prior to joining Evercore. Dillon is also a member of the board of directors of Caterpillar, Inc., Kellogg Company and DuPont. Senior managing director Richard Emerson boasts experience at Microsoft, where he served as senior vice president of corporate development and strategy, Lazard Freres and Morgan Stanley.

Visit Vault at www.vault.com for insider company profiles, expert advice,
career message boards, expert resume reviews, the Vault Job Board and more.

VAULT CAREER LIBRARY

45

Venturing out

Evercore Ventures' typical investments range from $1 million to $5 million. The arm focuses on companies in the communications, data storage, enterprise software, technology services and wireless sectors. Past investments include Atheros Communications, a semiconductor company that develops WiFi chipsets, and LowerMyBills.com, an Internet-based direct marketing and lead generation company. Both investments were realized in 2005.

Going public?

In July 2005, *The Daily Deal* published an article ("Evercore For Evermore") speculating that the firm may be gearing up to go public. Spurring the rumors are two recent hires, Fred Reynolds, a Viacom veteran who came on board as president, chief operating officer and chief financial officer, and Jane Wheeler, a Morgan Stanley alum who is now a senior managing director. Reynolds' high-level administrative experience (25 years as a CFO) would certainly be of use in the event of an IPO, as would Wheeler's background as a financial institutions group banker. Insiders say based on estimated revenue in 2004 of $110 million, Evercore would probably fetch a valuation of more than $700 million. For now, one thing is certain: Reynolds plans to dedicate his time to operations, investments and international expansion.

Ascent into the big leagues

Evercore's advisory business had a break-out year in 2004, surging up the M&A league tables in a way that defied expectation and, for some, belief. According to Thomson Financial, Evercore finished No. 12 in announced U.S. M&A, advising on 13 deals worth $58.1 billion, ranking first among boutique firms and moving up 33 spots from its No. 45 place the previous year.

A number of prominent transactions played a role in Evercore's climb in the league table rankings. In February 2004, the firm advised SBC in subsidiary Cingular Wireless' $47 billion acquisition of AT&T Wireless. Evercore was enlisted again in January 2005 when SBC acquired AT&T directly for $22 billion. Evercore also advised PanAmSat in its April 2004 $4.1 billion sale to private equity firm KKR, and recently advised StorageTek on its $4.1 billion announced sale to Sun Microsystems. Key clients also include companies such as Dow Jones, EDS and General Mills, among others.

GETTING HIRED

Evercore Partners offers recent undergrads the chance to participate in its two-year analyst program, designed to provide a broad range of experience in strategic advisory, restructuring, mergers and acquisitions, and private equity investments. According to the firm, analysts get the opportunity to "assume as much responsibility as their capabilities will allow" and "work closely with blue-chip clients." Evercore also says applicants should expect to work on several projects concurrently and should possess the drive to learn quickly in a fast-paced and dynamic environment. Experienced hires are encouraged to apply as well. The firm wants "top-tier" talent to join its offices in New York, Los Angeles and San Francisco.

Visit Vault at **www.vault.com** for insider company profiles, expert advice, career message boards, expert resume reviews, the Vault Job Board and more.

VAULT CAREER LIBRARY   47

Forstmann Little & Co.

767 Fifth Avenue
New York, NY
Phone: (212) 355-5656
Fax: (212) 759-9059

THE STATS

Senior Partner: Theodore J. Forstmann
Employer Type: Private Company

KEY COMPETITORS

Hicks Muse
KKR
Thomas H. Lee Partners

EMPLOYMENT CONTACT

Phone: (212) 355-5656

THE SCOOP

Big trouble

Founded in 1978, buyout firm Forstmann Little & Co. has been involved in some big deals – including investments in Ziff-Davis, Gulfstream Aerospace and General Instrument – and counts among its former advisory board members some big names, including Secretary of Defense Donald Rumsfeld, Secretary of State Colin Powell, George Shultz and Henry Kissinger. In total, the private equity group has invested more than $10 billion in some 30 companies.

The company, which specializes in telecommunications, technology, education and health care, has also gotten itself into some big trouble. For nearly three years, the buyout firm was embroiled in litigation with the state of Connecticut over negligent investments in technology companies XO Communications and McLeod USA. In July 2004, the jury found that Forstmann Little had breached its contract with Connecticut's state pension by over-investing in XO Communications between 1999 and 2001. Despite the "guilty" ruling, the six-man jury panel did not award damages, saying that Connecticut had okayed the investment and the buyout firm had sought lawyers' advice on the investment decision. When Connecticut decided to appeal the decision, Forstmann decided to fork over $15 million rather than drag the suit out any further.

Back in the fray

In September 2004, with the Connecticut lawsuit behind it, Forstmann Little made headlines by announcing the acquisition of Cleveland-based sports-management and talent agency IMG for $750 million. The agency represents many of the world's greatest celebrities, including Derek Jeter, Tiger Woods and Heidi Klum. In the year since the acquisition, Forstmann has revamped the firm's management structure, appointed himself chairman, stocked the board of directors with industry titans and cut about 10 percent of IMG's staff. He also gave or sold equity to around 80 IMG executives in the hopes of keeping managers happy.

Last deal

Back in September 2004, when Forstmann Little snatched up IMG, insiders speculated that the purchase would be the buyout firm's last. At the time, founder and senior partner Theodore Forstmann publicly rejected such theories, saying that

Visit Vault at **www.vault.com** for insider company profiles, expert advice, career message boards, expert resume reviews, the Vault Job Board and more.

VAULT CAREER LIBRARY

49

although the group would not raise another fund, it still had more than $1.5 billion left in the hopper. As he told *BusinessWeek*, "That buys a lot of golf balls." In May 2005, however, Forstmann admitted that he had thought the IMG deal would be his last – but 24 Hour Fitness proved too good to pass up. Forstmann acquired the privately-owned chain of fitness clubs for $1.6 billion, leaving $400 million left in Forstmann's fund. The money will most likely be used for strategic acquisitions for 24 Hour Fitness or IMG.

GETTING HIRED

Forstmann Little & Co. doesn't have a web site. Individuals interested in working for the private equity group can contact the firm via telephone or check out financial job sites such as jobsinthemoney.com and glocap.com.

General Atlantic, LLC

3 Pickwick Plaza
Greenwich, CT 06830
Phone: (203) 629-8600
Fax: (203) 622-8818
www.generalatlantic.com

THE STATS

Chairman: Steve A. Denning
Employer Type: Private Company
No. of Employees: 145
No. of Offices: 11

KEY COMPETITORS

Institutional Venture Partners
Summit Partners
TA Associates

EMPLOYMENT CONTACT

Phone: (203) 629-8600
For additional contact information,
check the company web site at
www.generalatlantic.com

Visit Vault at **www.vault.com** for insider company profiles, expert advice,
career message boards, expert resume reviews, the Vault Job Board and more.

VAULT CAREER LIBRARY 51

THE SCOOP

The Atlantic and beyond

Greenwich, Conn.-based General Atlantic is a global private equity group with an exclusive focus on information technology. Founded in 1980, the firm first began to seek investments outside the U.S. in the 1990s. Since then, it has established offices in London, Dusseldorf, Hong Kong, Mumbai, Sao Paulo and Singapore. Today, nearly half of the firm's more than 50 portfolio investments are foreign companies. General Atlantic generally invests in eight to 12 companies per year, for an annual investment target of $1 billion. All in, the tech private equity group has around $10 billion in capital under management.

Succession plans

In February 2005, co-founder and chairman of the firm's executive committee Steven A. Denning was named chairman, and William E. Ford, a managing director and chairman of the firm's investment committee, was named president. The two newly-created positions reflect the company's succession plans – Denning will continue to oversee strategy and capital raising, while Ford will assume responsibility for the group's operations, continuing to manage its investment activities. Before joining General Atlantic in 1991, Ford was an investment banker with Morgan Stanley. He received his BA in Economics from Amherst and his MBA from Stanford.

In the same month, General Atlantic announced a name change. The company, previously known as General Atlantic Partners, dropped the "partners" to reflect the fact that it is a limited liability company, not a partnership.

In the pits

In September 2005, General Atlantic invested $135 million in a 10 percent stake in Nymex, the world's largest energy market, beating out rival buyout houses Blackstone Group and Battery Ventures. General Atlantic initially sought a 20 percent stake in the exchange, but agreed to a smaller chunk when it became clear Nymex would not give up a larger share. Nymex has resisted going public for fear that outside investors would replace the pits with an electronic infrastructure. The General Atlantic investment, however, is seen as the first step toward an IPO.

Other recent deals for General Atlantic include a majority stake in www.webloyalty.com, a provider of online marketing and subscription services (in

April 2005); a $127 million investment in Saxo Bank, a provider of investment banking services using state-of-the-art online trading technology (in June 2005); and the buyout of Dice Inc., a provider of online recruiting services for technology, engineering and security-cleared professionals (in August 2005).

GETTING HIRED

General Atlantic does not provide information about job opportunities on its web site. Interested individuals should contact the firm's offices directly.

Visit Vault at **www.vault.com** for insider company profiles, expert advice,
career message boards, expert resume reviews, the Vault Job Board and more.

VAULT CAREER LIBRARY   53

Goldman Sachs Capital Partners

85 Broad Street
New York, NY 10004
Phone: (212) 902-1000
Fax: (212) 902-3000
www.gs.com/pia

DEPARTMENTS*

Build-Ups
Expansion/Growth Investments
Leveraged Buyouts/Management
  Buyouts
Private Closely Held Companies
Recapitalizations
Restructurings & Special Situations
Venture Technology

*Investment areas

THE STATS

**Managing Director & Head of
Principal Investment Area:** Richard A.
Friedman
Employer Type: Division of Goldman
Sachs
No. of Employees: 100+
No. of Offices: 5

EMPLOYMENT CONTACT

For employment and application
information, visit Goldman Sachs'
career site at www.gs.com/careers

THE SCOOP

Strong arm of the big dog

Goldman Sachs Capital Partners is the private equity unit of New York-based investment banking powerhouse Goldman Sachs. GS Capital Partners, which has invested over $17 billion of equity in over 500 companies since 1986, has more than 100 professionals who work out of offices in New York, San Francisco, London, Hong Kong and Tokyo.

Currently, the unit is busy investing its $8.5 billion GS Capital Partners V fund, $2.5 billion of which it raised from parent Goldman Sachs. It's the unit's fifth fund dedicated to making privately negotiated equity investments, seeking long-term capital appreciation by participating in leveraged buyouts, recapitalizations and growth investments to fund acquisition or expansion. The previous GS Capital Partners 2000 was a $5.25 equity billion fund, about $1.6 billion of which was committed by Goldman Sachs and its employees.

GS Capital Partners has had its hands in numerous high-profile deals over the years. The unit has invested in Burger King, Polo Ralph Lauren, Atkins Nutritionals, BPC Holding Corp., and Yankees Entertainment and Sports Network, among many more companies. GS Capital Partners operates under Goldman Sachs' principal investment area (PIA) in its merchant banking division. Also falling under PIA is GS Mezzanine Partners, which operates the largest mezzanine fund in the world. To date, Goldman Sachs' PIA has formed 11 investment vehicles worth a total of $26 billion. For the third quarter of 2005, principal investments booked net revenue of $843 million.

Meet the parent

Considered Wall Street's preeminent investment banking firm, Goldman Sachs has an unparalleled history of long-lasting success, rooted in a distinct business culture in which individual achievements are subordinate to the good of the firm. This, along with its longevity, has enabled Goldman to continuously attract and retain Wall Street's top talent, who year after year advise the world's largest companies on the largest mergers and acquisitions and underwriting deals. In 2004, Goldman ranked No. 1 in both announced and completed global M&A transactions, advising on seven of the 10 largest deals of the year and scoring a 30.5 percent market share in worldwide announced M&A, according to Thomson Financial.

Visit Vault at **www.vault.com** for insider company profiles, expert advice, career message boards, expert resume reviews, the Vault Job Board and more.

VAULT CAREER LIBRARY

55

In May 1999, the historically secretive and privately-held Goldman went public. During the year following the IPO, Goldman's stock gained 141 percent, outperforming nearly all of its competitors. In January 2004, *Investment Dealers Digest* reported that approximately 40 to 45 percent of Goldman stock was held by employees or former employees of Goldman, a much higher percentage than other investment banks.

Goldman's business is divided into three core sectors: investment banking, trading and principal investments, and asset management and securities services. The investment banking sector is further subdivided in two sectors: financial advisory and underwriting. The trading and principal investments business is subdivided into three categories: fixed income, currency and commodities, and equities and principal investments (under which GS Capital Partners falls). The asset management and securities services branch is also divided into three categories: asset management, securities services and commissions; as of August 2005, the firm's asset management unit managed $520 billion in assets. Headquartered in New York, Goldman has a worldwide presence, with additional offices in London, Frankfurt, Tokyo, Hong Kong and other major financial centers.

Recent big buys

In September 2005, a consortium of private equity firms, including GS Capital Partners, the Blackstone Group and DLJ Merchant Banking, announced its intention to acquire Texas-based insurer UICI, committing to invest over $1 billion of equity in the transaction. A month earlier, in August 2005, a Silver Lake Partners-led consortium of private equity firms, which included GS Capital Partners, acquired SunGard Data Systems for $11.4 billion in cash. The deal was the largest technology privatization ever completed, and the second largest leveraged buyout ever completed. Also in August, an investor group comprising Goldman Sachs Capital Partners, Kohlberg Kravis Roberts & Co. (KKR) and Five Mile Capital Partners agreed to buy a 60 percent interest in GMAC Commercial Holding Corp., the commercial mortgage subsidiary of General Motors Acceptance Corporation.

Prior to that, in June 2005, GS Capital Partners announced another big deal, agreeing to buy Pirelli's Energy and Telecom Cables and Systems business for about € 1.3 billion, which included intellectual property rights and Pirelli brand licensing for two years. Under the terms of the deal, GS Capital Partners will takeover Pirelli activities that booked sales of €3.2 billion in 2004 and operating income of more than €110 million. The business has 12,000 employees and 52 plants throughout the world.

GETTING HIRED

Candidates can check out the careers site of www.gs.com to find information about private equity jobs at Goldman Sachs. Undergraduates and advanced degree students join the firm through its merchant banking division (under which falls the principal investment area and, under that, GS Capital Partners). Undergrads join as analysts, advanced degree holders as associates. According to the firm, both analysts and associates will be involved in all areas of private equity investing, including "analyzing macro and microeconomic opportunities and risks inherent in specific countries, industries, companies and real estate assets; structuring and executing complex private equity investments, including detailed financial analysis, deal negotiation and transaction execution; assisting portfolio company management and operating partners to grow their businesses or real estate portfolios, typically through representation on the board of directors; and assessing the appropriate time to harvest an investment."

On the careers section of its web site, Goldman Sachs provides a list of upcoming on-campus recruiting events, descriptions of days in the life of current employees, links to online applications and interviewing tips, among other information.

Visit Vault at **www.vault.com** for insider company profiles, expert advice,
career message boards, expert resume reviews, the Vault Job Board and more.

VAULT CAREER LIBRARY   57

Hicks, Muse, Tate & Furst

200 Crescent Court
Suite 1600
Dallas, TX 75201
Phone: (214) 740-7300
Fax: (214) 720-7888
www.hmtf.com

THE STATS

Chairman: John R. Muse
Employer Type: Private Company
No. of Employees: 15
No. of Offices: 3

KEY COMPETITORS

Investcorp
KKR
Thomas H. Lee Partners

EMPLOYMENT CONTACT

Phone: (214) 740-7300

THE SCOOP

Buy and build

Hicks, Muse, Tate & Furst can trace its roots back to a hot tub in Snowmass, Colo. There, co-founders John Muse and Tom Hicks first discussed the idea of starting what would become one of the largest buyout firms in the U.S. Although the firm today is not as large as it once was, the Dallas-based private equity group is still a force to be reckoned with, with more than 400 completed transactions worth over $50 billion. The firm officially opened for business in 1989; today it has total funds managed of over $10 billion.

Hicks Muse targets underperforming companies in specific industry sectors – including media, consumer products, energy, financial services, information services and nice manufacturing – and pursues a "buy-and-build" investment strategy. In other words, the group acquires struggling companies, builds them up, and then uses them as a hub for further investments in the sector.

Something to Muse over

At the end of 2004, co-founder and former chairman Tom Hicks retired, handing over the reins to John Muse (of hot tub renown). A Texas native, Muse served in the Air Force for four years, earned his MBA from UCLA, and once harbored dreams of becoming an astronaut (but couldn't hack the hard math). Before joining forces with Hicks, Muse worked in investment banking as senior vice president and director of Schneider, Bernet & Hickman and then as head of investment and merchant banking for Prudential Securities' Southwest. Muse says his management style is pretty similar to Hicks' – only more low profile.

Slimming down

The past couple of years have been tough ones for Hicks Muse. The firm closed its office in Mexico City after investing around $1.5 billion in Latin America during the region's heyday, suffered losses from failed telecom investments and, most recently, lost its outpost in London. Formed seven years ago, the London office broke off from Hicks Muse in January 2005, later renaming itself Lion Capital to mark its independence. The only remaining tie between the two private equity firms is John Muse, who will remain on as non-executive chairman of the European group.

Visit Vault at **www.vault.com** for insider company profiles, expert advice, career message boards, expert resume reviews, the Vault Job Board and more.

VAULT CAREER LIBRARY   59

Still, if there's one thing Hicks Muse has learned it's that bigger is not necessarily better. As Muse told *The Dallas Morning News* in January 2005, "We realize we got our best performance when we were smaller." The firm's focus now is on doing mid-size deals, primarily in the areas of energy, food and media, which can deliver returns for investors. According to Muse, the group's $1.5 billion Fund V should achieve its 25 percent plus return targets, and a new fund is in the works for 2006.

Donut shopping

Hicks Muse isn't interested in billion-dollar deals these days – or is it? According to some industry observers, the private equity group has its eye on Dunkin' Brands, a unit of French drinks group Pernod. The division, which operates Dunkin' Donuts, Baskin Robbins and Togo's, is valued at more than $1.8 billion and has also (allegedly) attracted the attention of Bain Capital and The Carlyle Group. Pernod has hired JPMorgan to handle the sale.

Another noteworthy deal is the Dallas-based private equity group's acquisition of Swett & Crawford, the largest U.S. wholesale insurance brokerage firm from parent company Aon Corporation. Banc of America Capital Investors and Emerald Capital Group are also investors in the September 2005 deal, the financial terms of which were not disclosed. Earlier in the year, in May 2005, Hicks Muse acquired Sturm Foods, a Manawa, Wis.-based provider of dry mix products (drink mixes and hot cereals).

GETTING HIRED

Hicks, Muse, Tate & Furst employs a staff of 15, including five partners, one senior counselor, three principals, three analysts and three other professionals. The firm's web site does not provide career information, but individuals interested in working for the private equity group can contact the firm directly via phone or fax. Candidates might also consider scouring financial job sites or general job search engines.

Investcorp Corporate Investment

280 Park Avenue, 36th Floor
New York, NY 10017
Phone: (212) 599-4700
Fax: (212) 983-7073
www.investcorp.com

THE STATS

Head, North America: Christopher Stadler
Head, Europe: Steven Puccinelli
Employer Type: Subsidiary of Investcorp Bank BSC
No. of Employees: 39
No. of Offices: 2

KEY COMPETITORS

CD&R
KKR
Texas Pacific Group

EMPLOYMENT CONTACT

New York: (212) 599-4700
London: +44 (0)20 7629 6600

Visit Vault at **www.vault.com** for insider company profiles, expert advice, career message boards, expert resume reviews, the Vault Job Board and more.

VAULT CAREER LIBRARY   61

THE SCOOP

From A to Saks

Investcorp Corporate Investment is the private equity arm of Investcorp Bank BSC. (Investcorp Bank's other divisions include real estate investment, technology investment and asset management.) Although the parent company is headquartered in Bahrain, the Corporate Investment division is based in New York and has an additional outpost in London. From these two locations, the firm invests in mid-sized companies (in the range of $100 million to $1 billion) in North America and Europe. Investcorp chooses businesses with a good market position and strong track record, from luxury companies like Saks, Tiffany and Gucci to the less-glamorous Circle K, Simmons and Leica Geosystems. The group's current portfolio includes 23 companies.

Bought and sold

In fiscal 2005, Investcorp invested $800 million in five new acquisitions and generated $700 million in exit proceeds. The corporate investment group acquired Thomson Media, now called SourceMedia, a B2B provider of multimedia information; Associated Materials, the Ohio-based distributor of exterior residential building products; American Tire, the leading national tire distributor; Global Promo Group, a provider of specialty advertising and promotional products; and Polyconcept, a promotional, lifestyle and gift products provider. On the other end, the team sold three previous investments – MW Manufacturers, Gerresheimer and ECI – and recapitalized Hilding Anders, Stahl, PlayPower and Welcome Break.

Expert advice

Investcorp's staff includes 32 investment professionals who conduct due diligence, monitor portfolio companies and assist management teams, as well as seven advisory directors – former and current executives who bring decades of industry experience to the table. The advisory "board" includes experts in the automotive, industrial, manufacturing, media, retail and telecommunications sectors. These directors are available to portfolio companies to provide assistance in areas such as strategic assessment, identification of new business opportunities and cash flow improvement, among others.

GETTING HIRED

Investcorp does not provide employment information on its web site. Candidates interested in finding out more about job opportunities should contact the firm's New York or London office.

Visit Vault at **www.vault.com** for insider company profiles, expert advice, career message boards, expert resume reviews, the Vault Job Board and more.

VAULT CAREER LIBRARY   63

J.W. Childs Associates, LP

111 Huntington Avenue
Suite 2900
Boston, MA 02199-7610
Phone: (617) 753-1100
Fax: (617) 753-1101
www.jwchilds.com

THE STATS

President: John W. Childs
Employer Type: Private Company
No. of Employees: 29
No. of Offices: 3

KEY COMPETITORS

Blackstone Group
Hicks Muse
Texas Pacific Group

EMPLOYMENT CONTACT

Boston: (617) 753-1100
Hong Kong: (852) 2844-1950
Shanghai: (8621) 5877-8100

THE SCOOP

Childs' play

Founded in 1995 by four Thomas H. Lee expats, J.W. Childs Associates specializes in leveraged buyouts and recapitalizations of middle-market growth companies – specifically, ones with an enterprise value of around $150 to $600 million that have the capacity for operating earnings growth of more than 10 percent per year. To narrow down the field even further, J.W. Childs focuses on just three industries: consumer products, health care and specialty retail. The Boston-based firm has invested some $7 billion to date and seeks to make between eight and 12 new investments per year (for a total value of approximately $1 billion). Its current portfolio includes menswear line Joseph Abboud, Pinnacle Foods, NutraSweet, Sunny Delight Beverages, Equinox Fitness Clubs and Sheridan Healthcare.

Vested

Once J.W. Childs invests in a company, the firm wants a senior management team that is vested in the performance of the company. In order to align the interests of J.W. Childs and management teams, the private equity group offers managers the opportunity to purchase a stake in the buyout. In keeping with this philosophy of common interests, the buyout firm's professionals have been known to commit personal capital alongside management and the investment fund. To date, J.W. Childs' professionals have invested $115 million in portfolio companies.

Operating expertise

Like other private equity firms, J.W. Childs has accumulated a panel of experts, known as Operating Partners, to call on for help throughout the life of an investment, from due diligence to portfolio oversight (roles range from active member of the board of directors to non-executive chairman of the board). The firm's operating partners have operating experience with major U.S. corporations, including Baxter Healthcare, Best Foods, Caremark International, General Electric, General Foods, General Nutrition Companies, Procter & Gamble and Sears Roebuck. What's more, each partner has been the CEO of a successful middle-market leveraged buyout or privately held company.

Visit Vault at **www.vault.com** for insider company profiles, expert advice, career message boards, expert resume reviews, the Vault Job Board and more.

VAULT CAREER LIBRARY

65

Asian acquisitions

Based in Boston, J.W. Childs has additional offices in Hong Kong and Shanghai. Through these outposts, J.W. Childs can scout out potential acquisition targets in Asia and work with portfolio companies interested in international expansion and outsourcing opportunities. Kam Son Leong is the managing director of the firm's Asian operations.

New deal

The private equity group's most recent acquisition is the $400 million buyout of Brookstone, a developer and retailer of specialty home gadgets. The investment team on that deal also included OSIM International, a Singapore-based vendor of healthy lifestyle products; Temasek Holdings, a private equity firm in Singapore; and a handful of Brookstone executives. The Merrimack, N.H.-based company operates 292 stores in the U.S. and Puerto Rico.

GETTING HIRED

J.W. Childs does not provide career information on its web site. Individuals interested in working for the private equity group should contact the firm directly at its offices in Boston, Hong Kong or Shanghai.

JPMorgan Partners

1221 Avenue of the Americas
New York, NY 10020
Phone: (212) 899-3400
Fax: (212) 899-3401
www.jpmorganpartners.com

DEPARTMENTS

Asia
Europe
Latin America
North America

THE STATS

Managing Partner: Jeffrey C. Walker
Employer Type: Unit of JPMorgan
Chase*
No. of Employees: 150
No. of Offices: 9

*After JPMorgan Partners
completes the investment of its
current $6.5 billion Global Fund, it
will become an independent
company.

KEY COMPETITORS

KKR
New Enterprise Associates
Summit Partners

EMPLOYMENT CONTACT

E-mail:
resumes@jpmorganpartners.com

Visit Vault at **www.vault.com** for insider company profiles, expert advice,
career message boards, expert resume reviews, the Vault Job Board and more.

VAULT CAREER LIBRARY   67

THE SCOOP

Going solo

JPMorgan Partners (JPMP) is currently the private equity arm of the monstrous financial services firm JPMorgan Chase, but soon it will be going solo. In March 2005, the firm's parent announced that JPMP, after it completes the investment of its current $6.5 billion Global Fund, will become an independent company. "Over the last 21 years, JPMorgan Partners has successfully built a world-class, globally integrated, private equity franchise," said David Coulter, vice chairman of JPMorgan Chase, in a press release. "We want them to continue to grow and deepen that organization. They and we have determined that they can best achieve their desired scale independent of JPMorgan Chase."

As of June 30, 2005, JPMP had over $11 billion in capital under management, and since its founding in 1984, the firm has closed more than 1,300 transactions, investing over $15 billion in consumer, media, energy, industrial, financial services, health care, hardware and software companies. Like its parent, JPMP is based in New York, and some of its 95-plus employees also work out of offices in San Francisco, London, Mexico City, Sao Paolo, Buenos Aires, Munich, Hong Kong and Tokyo. JPMP's portfolio companies include AMC Entertainment, Berry Plastics, Cabela's, Pinnacle Foods, PQ Corporation, SafetyKleen Europe, Vetco International and Warner Chilcott.

Investing abroad

JPMorgan Partners' European operation is located in two offices, in London and Munich. In Europe, JPMP specializes in middle-market buyouts, targeting companies with enterprise values between €150 million and €750 million. The firm focuses on investments in manufacturing, chemicals, health care and packaging.

In Asia, JPMP manages the $1.1 billion Asia Opportunity Fund, its sole investment vehicle in the continent, and the largest direct equity investment fund focusing on Asia. In Latin America, JPMP has 15 employees, who operate out of offices in Buenos Aires, Mexico City and São Paulo. The JPMP Latin America team manages a portfolio of more than 50 companies, valued at approximately $485 million of assets.

The parental unit (for the time being)

J.P. Morgan Chase & Co. (known informally as JPMorgan Chase) takes its name from the massive merger between two diversified financial institutions with long histories. JPMorgan traces its roots back to 1838, when American George Peabody opened a London merchant bank. Chase Manhattan's history can be traced back to 1799, when Chase's first predecessor firm, The Manhattan Company, was chartered to supply water to New York City. The merger between the two, valued at approximately $38.6 billion, was completed on the first day of 2001, instantly creating the third-largest financial institution in terms of assets in the U.S., behind Citigroup and Bank of America.

Less than four years later, the firm went big again. On July 1, 2004, JPMorgan Chase officially merged with Bank One Corporation for a purchase price of $58.5 billion. Upon the merger, the combined company possessed $1.1 trillion in assets, rivaling Citigroup's $1.2 trillion. The deal was one of the largest financial mergers in U.S. history and extended JPMorgan Chase's domestic reach beyond the East Coast. The new entity offers a combined 2,300 branches in 17 states in the Midwest and Southwest. It also services approximately 87 million credit cards. The acquisition of Bank One is expected to boost JPMorgan Chase's ability to compete with Citigroup not only in investment banking and commercial lending, but also in consumer banking, which is Bank One's key strength. The combined entity is headquartered in New York, but retail operations, excluding credit cards, are run out of Chicago.

JPMorgan Chase conducts most of its investment banking operations under the JPMorgan name and most of its commercial banking operations under the Chase name. The company can be further broken down into six major business units: investment banking, retail financial services, card services, commercial banking, treasury and securities services, asset and wealth management, and corporate.

Big scores

In December 2004, JPMorgan Partners agreed to acquire PQ Corporation, a privately-held chemicals and engineered glass materials company. Prior to that, in August 2004, JPMP invested $25 million in College Sports Television, comprised of two main units: College Sports TV and College Sports.com. College Sports TV televises regular season and championship gmaes from every major collegiate athletic conference, in addition to nine NCAA Championships. CollegeSports.com is the most-trafficked college sports web site, and its network of nearly 160 official athletic sites are top sources for college sports broadband content, news, information, scores and analysis. Also investing $12 million in CSTV at the time were the New York City Investment Fund and several existing CSTV investors, including Constellation Ventures, Allen & Co. and the Coca-Cola Company. Following the deal, JPMP and fellow private investment firm Apollo Management owned 50.1 percent of CSTV.

GETTING HIRED

Candidates interested in positions at JPMP (or at one of the its portfolio companies) can e-mail their resume as a Word document attachment to resumes@jpmorganpartners.com. According to JPMP, "A member of our team may be in touch with you if your background matches any current opportunities."

Kohlberg Kravis Roberts & Co. (KKR)

9 West 57th Street
Suite 4200
New York, NY 10019
Phone: (212) 750-8300
Fax: (212) 750-0003
www.kkr.com

THE STATS

Founding Partners: Henry Kravis & George Roberts
Employer Type: Private Company
No. of Employees: 60
No. of Offices: 3

KEY COMPETITORS

CD&R
Forstmann Little
Hicks Muse

EMPLOYMENT CONTACT

New York: (212) 750-8300
Menlo Park: (650) 233-6560
London: 44 207 839 9800

Visit Vault at **www.vault.com** for insider company profiles, expert advice,
career message boards, expert resume reviews, the Vault Job Board and more.

VAULT CAREER LIBRARY   71

THE SCOOP

Head honcho

Kohlberg Kravis Roberts & Co., commonly known as KKR, is the recognized leader in the private equity world. Founded in 1976, the firm quickly built a reputation for itself as both innovator and head honcho. Its achievements include the first billion-dollar buyout transaction, two of the largest buyout transactions ever (RJR Nabisco and Beatrice for $31.4 billion and $8.7 billion, respectively), the largest buyout in France and two of the largest Canadian buyouts. All in, KKR has completed more than 130 transactions worth $162 billion. The private equity guru employs 60 professionals based in New York, Menlo Park and London. Of these, 16 are what the firm calls "members," who have an average of 16 years with the firm.

The KKR way

So what's the secret behind KKR's success? For one, the firm has a long-standing reputation that works to its advantage when going after deals. KKR also boasts a network of relationships in "Main Street" industries and throughout Wall Street. Diversification is another key factor for the private equity group, which has invested in both fledgling start-ups and established corporations, traditional industries and less conventional sectors. The firm's industry experience includes chemicals, communications, consumer products, energy, financial services, health care, homebuilding, hospitality and leisure, industrial and manufacturing, media and retail. Yet another reason for KKR's success is its long-term view; the firm's average investment period is seven years, although the firm has held a handful of companies for more than 10 years. Finally, KKR brings a certain level of expertise to the table in terms of managing its portfolio companies. This know-how includes the ability to attract strong management, "incentivize" management and employees, pursue acquisitions and divestitures, arrange financings, provide effective oversight and maximize value when exiting investments.

The next frontier

Asia is one arena in which KKR is not the top dog. While competitors like the Carlyle Group have been in Asia since the late 1990s, KKR has yet to get into the mix. All that is about to change, however. In September 2005, the private equity leader announced plans to open up offices in Hong Kong and Tokyo by the end of the year. Joseph Y. Bae, now a Managing Director in KKR's New York office, will make the transition to Hong Kong and head up the firm's operations in Asia. Justin Reizes, a principal from the firm's London outpost, will join Bae.

The private equity firm's European division, on the other hand, has been busy. The London-based team snatched up five companies in 2004, worth a total of $9.8 billion. And one of the group's earliest acquisitions, banking information systems specialist Wincor Nixdorf, has staged a remarkable turnaround. Wincor more than doubled its workers after KKR took over in 1999, and the company recently ranked No. 8 in German job creation between 2000 and 2005. Still, KKR would do well to proceed with caution in Germany, as the current attitude toward foreign buyout firms is none too friendly. Franz Muntefering, chairman of the Social Democrats, likened private equity firms such as KKR to "swarms of locusts sucking the substance" from German companies.

Toy story

August 2005 was a busy month for KKR. The private equity group teamed up with Silver Lake Partners to acquire Agilent's semiconductor business for $2.65 billion and partnered with Permira to buy SBS Broadcasting S.A. for approximately $2.55 billion. The firm also announced plans to acquire a 60 percent interest in the financial services subsidiary of General Motors, known as GMAC, and saw the completion of the record-breaking $11.3 billion SunGard Data Systems deal.

Although July 2005 was a bit tamer compared to August, the month marked the completion of the $6.6 billion acquisition of Toys R Us. Originally, KKR had planned to go it alone, targeting the retailers toy business by itself, but later joined forces with Bain Capital Partners and Vornado Realty Trust to buy the whole company (including its baby-products stores). Experts say part of the retailer's appeal is its real estate, which includes 1,500 stores around the world, with 681 in the U.S. One option for the new owners is to close down these stores and rent the space to fast-growing chains like Lowes, Bed Bath & Beyond and Target, or to sell the properties outright.

While stockholders clearly had faith that the takeover was a good thing for the company (the stock increased dramatically prior to the completion of the deal), others remain skeptical about the investors' ability to turn things around. For one, Toys R Us faces increasing competition from the likes of Wal-Mart and Target. Furthermore, the bricks and mortar retailer has yet to find an online strategy that works.

On the selling block?

Specialty publishing and targeted media company Primedia is one of KKR's longest running investments. The private equity group has made a number of investments, dating back to 1989 when Primedia was first getting its feet on the ground. In fact, the media company was originally known as K-III Communications, reflecting the start-up's financial backers (KKR). As of late, Primedia has been engaged in a fair amount of buying and selling, beefing up its portfolio of magazines, while selling off key assets. The largest sale came in February 2005, when Primedia sold its About.com web site to The New York Times Company. Other recent transactions include the sale of Bankers Training & Consulting Company to BAI in March 2005, the acquisition of the Auto Interiors Exposition & Conference from VNU in April 2005, and the purchase of NHU Publishing in May 2005. In April 2005, the media company also announced that it is contemplating the sale of its business information segment. According to Primedia president and chief executive, Kelly Conlin, the business information division has experienced accelerated revenue and earnings growth, attracting a host of potential buyers. Insiders speculate that all this activity means KKR may finally be getting ready to put this portfolio company up for sale.

Defectors at the gate

KKR prides itself on a low turnover rate among its employees, which is why the firm was none too pleased when two of its brightest stars, Scott Stuart and Edward Gilhuly, announced their departure in September 2005. The two partners left the firm in order to start their own investment fund. Insiders suspect that the move may have been triggered by the founding generation's reluctance to give up the reins. KKR is run by Henry Kravis and George Roberts, both 61 with no plans to retire, and is considered one of the most closely controlled private equity firms in the business. Stuart and Gilhuly, roommates at Stanford Business School, told *The Wall Street Journal* that their departure had nothing to do with the founding partners, describing Kravis and Roberts as "fully engaged and the right guys to run KKR."

GETTING HIRED

KKR does not provide employment information on its web site. Candidates interested in working for the private equity firm should contact the firm directly at its offices in New York, Menlo Park and London.

Lehman Brothers Private Equity

745 Seventh Avenue
New York, NY 10019
Phone: (212) 526-7000
Fax: (212) 526-8766
www.lehman.com/im/pe

DEPARTMENTS

Fixed Income Related Investments
Merchant Banking
Private Fund Investments
Private Fund Marketing Group
Real Estate
Venture Capital

THE STATS

Managing Director & Head of Private Equity: Michael J. Odrich
Employer Type: Unit of Lehman Brothers
No. of Offices: 6

Visit Vault at **www.vault.com** for insider company profiles, expert advice, career message boards, expert resume reviews, the Vault Job Board and more.

VAULT CAREER LIBRARY   75

THE SCOOP

Twenty years strong

Founded in 1984, Lehman Brothers Private Equity manages a number of private equity portfolios, with approximately $10 billion in assets under management. Based in New York, the unit of international banking giant Lehman Brothers has five main divisions: merchant banking, venture capital, real estate, fixed income related investments and private funds investments. The Lehman Brothers Merchant Banking Partners III L.P. fund has $1.2 billion in committed capital and currently holds investment positions in several companies, including Antero Resources, Hunter Fan Company, Phoenix Brands LLC, Industria de Turbo Propulsores and LB Pacific LP. One of the fund's most recent deals came in September 2005, when it agreed to acquire the Spumador Group, a family-owned Italian branded and private label soft drink and mineral water bottling business, with annual revenue of about €150 million.

To date, Lehman Brothers' Venture Capital has approximately $1.1 billion in total capital, with $717 million invested in more than 80 portfolio companies. The group has offices in New York, Silicon Valley and Los Angeles. Lehman Brothers Real Estate Partners is a merchant banking fund with total committed capital of $1.6 billion. The fund invests in properties, real estate companies and service businesses ancillary to the real estate industry, placing money into opportunities in North America, Europe and other international markets. Investments typically range between $10 million and $100 million. The division has committed over $1.3 billion in equity in 49 transactions.

Parent on a roll

Lehman Brothers (Lehman Brothers Private Equity's parent) followed a strong 2003 with a stronger 2004, booking record net revenue and net income, and finishing in the top five of several important investment banking league tables. Net revenue increased 34 percent to $11.6 billion, and net income increased 39 percent to $2.4 billion. Its investment banking segment also earned record net revenue, as did its capital markets business unit, with the fixed income division posting its fifth consecutive year of record net revenue and the equity division its second best year of net revenue. According to Thomson Financial, Lehman Brothers scored a No. 2 and No. 3 ranking in U.S. completed M&A and U.S. announced M&A, respectively.

Lehman's profitability and success aren't anything new. After its spin off from American Express in the mid-1990s, Lehman posted solid results in the late 1990s and early part of the new millennium. Expanding over the last 154 years, the company is a full-service global investment bank providing a wide range of financial services, including fixed income and equity underwriting, sales, trading, research, M&A advisory, public finance, private investment management, asset management and private equity. Lehman attributes its success to its culture, teamwork and "the longest serving executive team on Wall Street, with over 200 years of combined tenure."

The principals' office

Michael J. Odrich, head of Lehman Brothers Private Equity and partner in Lehman Brothers Venture Partners, joined the private equity unit in 1995, the same year he founded Lehman Brothers' venture investment program. Prior to joining Lehman Brothers Private Equity, he spent three years as a senior advisor to parent Lehman Brothers' chairman and CEO, and was involved in strategic and financial planning, board of directors matters, management of Lehman Brothers' worldwide business, and merchant banking and investment banking transactions. Odrich joined the investment banking division of Lehman Brothers in 1986, spending most of his time in the M&A department until becoming a senior advisor.

Charles Ayres, global head of merchant banking, has more than 19 years of private equity experience. In 2003, he joined Lehman from MidOcean Partners where he was a founding partner. Previously he was head of Deutsche Bank's DB Capital Partners and a member of the DB Americas Regional Executive Committee. Javier Bañon, a principal of the merchant banking group who heads up the London-based part of that group, was previously a managing director at DB Capital Partners. He joined Lehman in 2004.

GETTING HIRED

At the "careers" section of www.lehman.com, candidates can check out the firm's on-campus recruiting schedule, details on each unit within Lehman Brothers Private Equity and first-person accounts of life at Lehman, among other hiring information. Recruiting for private equity analysts and associates, both summer and full-time, is done in conjunction with Lehman Brothers' investment banking recruiting. All analysts and associates begin their positions with a training program (the length of which varies according to position and level). Summer analysts and summer associates perform similar duties as full-time hires.

Madison Dearborn Partners, LLC

3 First National Plaza, Suite 3800
Chicago, IL 60602
Phone: (312) 895-1000
Fax: (312) 895-1001
www.mdcp.com

THE STATS

Chairman & CEO: John A. Canning, Jr.
Employer Type: Private Company
No. of Employees: 35
No. of Offices: 1

KEY COMPETITORS

Bain Capital
Platinum Equity
Safeguard Scientifics

EMPLOYMENT CONTACT

Phone: (312) 895-1000

Visit Vault at **www.vault.com** for insider company profiles, expert advice,
career message boards, expert resume reviews, the Vault Job Board and more.

VAULT CAREER LIBRARY   79

THE SCOOP

Good old boys

Although Madison Dearborn Partners (MDP) got its start in 1993, the private equity firm's principals have been in cahoots since the 1980s when they built a $2.6 billion management buyout and venture capital portfolio at First Chicago Corporation. Today, this tightly knit group has an average tenure of 13 years and a personal investment in each of the firm's transactions. The Chicago-based company manages four funds worth nearly $8 billion, the most recent of which is a $4 billion fund launched in 2001. Madison Dearborn focuses on management buyouts and growth equity investments in five primary industries: basic industries, communications, consumer, financial services and health care. Recent additions to the firm's portfolio of 56 companies include wireless communications service provider MetroPCS Communications for $738 million in October 2005 and German dental equipment maker Sirona Dental Systems for $1.03 billion in May 2005. MCP investments typically range from $100 to $600 million.

Sizzling

In 1999, Madison Dearborn Partners led the buyout of Ruth's Chris Steak House. The company's shaky financial results coupled with a balance sheet burdened with debt made insiders skeptical about the success of the planned IPO. But in August 2005, the restaurant chain's IPO sizzled – at least relative to expectations. Ruth's Chris sold 13 million shares at $18 per share for a total of $234 million, more than $50 million more than experts speculated the company would raise. The IPO was a boon for Madison Dearborn, whose initial investment of $47 million is now worth around $240 million.

The paper chase

Madison Dearborn has an affinity for paper products companies. Its first foray into the industry, the $2.7 billion buyout of Riverwood International Corp. in 1996, was a flop. But the private equity firm learned from its mistakes, and its next venture, the $2.2 billion purchase of Packaging Corp. of America (PCA) in 1999, proved to be a staggering success. In 2000, Madison Dearborn took the company public at $12 a share and, by January 2004, the stock had jumped to $22, making the private equity firm's initial investment of $208 million worth $970 million.

The firm's next deal, the buyout of Jefferson Smurfit, the No. 1 European maker of containerboard and corrugated products, has hit some snafus. The portfolio company has not produced significant revenue growth due to a weak paper products market in Europe and, although the private equity group has reduced debt significantly, experts say the key to the firm's investment is expanding the top line.

Madison Dearborn's most recent paper products investment, Boise Cascade, seemed likely to be another winner for the private equity group. The buyout firm purchased the paper, forest products and timberland assets of Boise Cascade Corp. in October 2004 for around $3.9 billion. Madison Dearborn and management pumped some $250 million into the timberland business and sold that unit off to Forest Capital Partners for $1.7 billion in February 2005. The remaining business was scheduled to go public at a price range of $24 to $26 per share, which would make Madison Dearborn's stake worth roughly $1.3 billion, or four times its initial investment. But in May 2005, the IPO was cancelled (or at least delayed) due to an unreceptive market.

GETTING HIRED

Madison Dearborn does not provide career information on its web site. Candidates can contact the firm directly at its headquarters in Chicago.

Visit Vault at **www.vault.com** for insider company profiles, expert advice,
career message boards, expert resume reviews, the Vault Job Board and more.

VAULT CAREER LIBRARY   81

Onex Corporation

712 Fifth Avenue
New York, NY 10019
Phone: (212) 582-2211
Fax: (212) 582-0909
www.onexcorp.com

THE STATS

Chairman, President & CEO: Gerald
W. Schwartz
Employer Type: Public Company
No. of Employees: 22 (professionals)
No. of Offices: 2

KEY COMPETITORS

Counsel Corporation
Heico Companies
Thomas H. Lee Partners

EMPLOYMENT CONTACT

info@onex.com

THE SCOOP

O Canada

Founded in 1983, the Onex Corporation may not be the biggest name in private equity, but the Toronto-based firm is making big strides. For starters, in February 2004, the buyout house closed its $2 billion Onex Partners fund. And in January 2005, Onex Real Estate Partners, a $200 fund dedicated to acquiring real estate in North America, was born. Then in February 2005, Onex completed the acquisition of two health care companies, American Medical Response (AMR) and EmCare Holdings, for approximately $1 billion. Most recently, in July 2005, the group invested $1.5 billion in the Wichita/Tulsa division of Boeing Commercial Airplanes.

Eight is enough

Onex portfolio companies fall into eight industries: electronic manufacturing services; theatre exhibition; health care; customer management services; automotive products; personal care products; communications infrastructure; and small-capitalization opportunities. In 2004, the Canadian buyout's portfolio companies posted strong financial results, boosting revenue 34 percent to $16.2 billion and turning a net loss of $331 million into a net gain of $35 million. During that year, the private equity group made four acquisitions, including Magellan Health Services in January; social services provider Res-Care in June; Compagnie Generale de Geophysique, a supplier of products and services to the oil and gas industries, in November; and outsourced supply chain management services provider Cosmetic Essence in December. Onex Corp. said the two primary drivers for the sales increase were higher revenue for electronics manufacturing services provider Celestica and the acquisition of Magellan Health Services.

Effective exits

Since its inception, Onex has delivered compound annual returns on invested capital of 29 percent. Recent success stories for the buyout firm include Celestica, a former IBM Canada subsidiary acquired by Onex in the mid-1990s, Magellan Health Services and truck components maker Commercial Vehicle Group. In May 2005, Onex sold shares in Celestica for a pre-tax gain of $189 million and announced that it would sell half its stake in Magellan Health Services for net proceeds of $180 million. In July 2005, the company completed the sale to the public of its remaining interest in Commercial Vehicle Group for a return of $89 million.

GETTING HIRED

Onex Corporation has offices in Toronto and New York. Candidates interested in working for the firm should e-mail their resume to info@onex.com.

Parthenon Capital

75 State Street
26th Floor
Boston, MA 02109
Phone: (617) 960-4000
Fax: (617) 960-4010
www.parthenoncapital.com

THE STATS

Co-Founders: Ernest K. Jacquet &
John C. Rutherford
Employer Type: Private Company
No. of Employees: 47
No. of Offices: 2

EMPLOYMENT CONTACT

Undergrads and MBAs
E-mail: mollyf@parthenoncapital.com
Senior management positions
E-mail: marshallb@parthenoncapital.com

Visit Vault at **www.vault.com** for insider company profiles, expert advice,
career message boards, expert resume reviews, the Vault Job Board and more.

VAULT CAREER LIBRARY

85

THE SCOOP

Monumental

Founded in 1998, Parthenon Capital is a $1.1 billion private equity firm focused on middle-market companies. The firm's team of 47 operates out of offices in Boston and San Francisco, typically making investments in the range of $20 million to $100 million.

Parthenon is a somewhat heady name for a company that lacks the size or the prominence of other private equity firms. But co-founders Ernest Jacquet and John Rutherford say they wanted something that implied power and endurance. And, according to an August 2005 article in *Buyouts* magazine, with four exits in 2005 alone, the firm is well on its way to establishing its name in the private equity business.

Full potential

Parthenon Capital helps its portfolio companies grow through its "full potential" approach. This method entails partnering with existing management teams to provide a full range of strategic and financial services, from executive search and market strategy to debt financing and add-on acquisitions. The private equity group also offers its portfolio companies deep industry knowledge in its areas of expertise: business and financial services; health care; consumer products; value-added distribution; food and beverage; and niche manufacturing. Finally, the buyout firm limits its focus to just a few companies so that it can be actively involved – but not heavy-handed.

Low-carb craze fizzles

When Parthenon Capital and Goldman Sachs Capital Partners paid $400 to $500 million for a majority stake in Atkins Nutritionals in October 2003, the company was in the midst of a sizzling growth spurt. In that year, the low-carb craze instigator doubled revenue and accounted for most of the growth in the entire food industry. Today, the entry of food giants Kraft Foods, Unilever and General Mills into the low-carb market has fizzled much of that sizzle. Experts say Atkins overpriced itself, believing it could continue to charge more than its competitors for the Atkins name. What's more, research firm NPD Group reported that low-carb diets peaked in February 2004, when around 9.1 percent of Americans adhered to the regimen; that figure fell to 2.2 percent by July 2005. This is bad news for Parthenon, which may lose most of its investment in the diet company.

Parthenon was much more successful with AccuMed Health, a provider of home nursing and physical therapy services. The private equity group invested $75 million in the company's recapitalization in September 2004 and, just over a year later, found a buyer in TLC Health Care Services. Other successful exits include Rackable Systems and Interline Brands, which went public in June 2005 and December 2004, respectively, and Arrow Financial Services and Spheris, which were sold in September 2004 and November 2004, respectively.

Investors back out

Still, when Parthenon asked limited partners to pitch in for a new $1 billion fund, it did not get the response it was hoping for. Although the firm's second fund is likely to produce quality returns in spite of Atkins, insiders say many Fund II investors will not return for Fund III. An existing Parthenon investor told *Buyouts* magazine in August 2005, "Atkins is a big issue for us, and I still don't know if we'll get over it. They continue to have positive exits that are going to make the current fund a top performer, but some of the decisions [regarding Atkins] might be too egregious to ignore."

GETTING HIRED

Parthenon Capital hires individuals with at least two years of investment banking or consulting experience for the associate position, and seeks MBA graduates for the position of vice president. Interested individuals can e-mail their resume to Molly Fazio at mollyf@parthenoncapital.com. Candidates seeking management positions should contact Marshall Bennett at marshallb@parthenoncapital.com.

Visit Vault at **www.vault.com** for insider company profiles, expert advice, career message boards, expert resume reviews, the Vault Job Board and more.

VAULT CAREER LIBRARY

87

Providence Equity Partners Inc.

50 Kennedy Plaza, 18th Floor
Providence, RI 02903
Phone: (401) 751-1700
Fax: (401) 751-1790
www.provequity.com

THE STATS

CEO: Jonathan M. Nelson
Employer Type: Private Company
No. of Employees: 39
No. of Offices: 3

KEY COMPETITORS

Bain Capital
Blackstone Group
KKR

EMPLOYMENT CONTACT

Providence: (401) 751-1700
New York: (212) 644-1200
London: +44 207 514 8800

THE SCOOP

Heavy hitter

With more than $9 billion in capital under management, Providence Equity Partners counts itself among private equity's heavy hitters. Founded in 1991, the Providence, R.I.-based firm targets media and communications companies at varying stages of development. To date, the group has invested in more than 80 companies operating in 20 countries, with a current portfolio that includes Nextel, T-Mobile and Casema (the No. 3 cable operator in the Netherlands). Providence's staff of 39 operates out of offices in Providence, New York and London.

Dealmaker

Providence Equity Partners has been busy as of late. In April, the private equity group teamed up with Sony to lead the $5 billion acquisition of Metro-Goldwyn-Meyer (MGM). Providence also had its hands in the year's biggest deal, the $11.3 buyout of SunGard Data Systems in August 2005. In the same month, the firm joined forces with Apax Partners, Permira Advisors and the Blackstone Group to make a bid for TDC, Denmark's largest telecommunications carrier, with a market value of $9 billion. Other recent acquisitions include telecommunications software and services business Telcordia Technologies, and Crown Media International, the owner and operator of the international versions of the Hallmark Channel. Both were acquired in March 2005.

An exception to Providence's recent winning streak is its bid, with KKR, for the bankrupt Adelphia Communications. The two private equity firms made a joint bid of $16 billion in February 2005, but were beat out by Comcast and Time Warner Cable, whose $18 billion offer was accepted in April.

Success stories

In addition to new transactions, Providence has made good on some of its previous investments. In August 2004, Providence teamed up with private equity bigwigs KKR and the Carlyle Group to acquire satellite operator PanAmSat for $2.6 billion. The private equity consortium made millions in March 2005 when they sold 42 percent of PanAmSat to the public for $2.9 billion. Then in August 2005, the group scored again when competitor Intelsat agreed to buy PanAmSat for $3.2 billion, representing a 40 percent premium over the company's IPO price of $18.

Visit Vault at **www.vault.com** for insider company profiles, expert advice, career message boards, expert resume reviews, the Vault Job Board and more.

VAULT CAREER LIBRARY

89

Yet another success story is the Warner Music Group (WMG). In February 2004, Providence joined forces with Thomas H. Lee and Bain Capital to purchase WMG and by the time the company went public in May 2005, the private equity firms had already realized their initial investment. And they may stand to gain even more. In a recent interview with *BusinessWeek*, Warner Music Group CEO Edgar Bronfman Jr. said the private equity groups don't have plans to exit any time soon, describing them as bullish on the company's future.

Power play

In August 2005, Michael K. Powell, the former chairman of the Federal Communications Commission, joined the Providence team in the role of senior advisor. Powell is exclusively affiliated with Providence in the private equity field and will contribute his expertise in technology and regulatory issues in the media, communications and information industries to both new opportunities and existing investments. Experts speculate that bringing Powell on board may be related to a new deal in the works, possibly the buyout of T-Mobile, which is currently owned by Deutsche Telekom.

GETTING HIRED

Providence Equity Partners does not provide career information on its web site. Candidates interested in working for the private equity group can contact the firm's offices in Providence, New York or London.

Silver Lake Partners

2725 Sand Hill Road, Suite 150
Menlo Park, CA 94025
Phone: (650) 233-8120
Fax: (650) 233-8125
www.slpartners.com

THE STATS

Founding Partner & Managing Director: James A. Davidson
Employer Type: Private Company
Revenue: $6.6 million (est.)
No. of Employees: 23
No. of Offices: 3

KEY COMPETITORS

Bain Capital
Blackstone Group
KKR

EMPLOYMENT CONTACT

West Coast office: (650) 233-8120
East Coast office: (212) 981-5600
London office: +44 207 409 5030

Visit Vault at **www.vault.com** for insider company profiles, expert advice,
career message boards, expert resume reviews, the Vault Job Board and more.

VAULT CAREER LIBRARY   91

THE SCOOP

Kings of technology

In 1997, David J. Roux, James A. Davidson, Roger McNamee and Glenn Hutchins banded together to form Silver Lake Partners, a private equity firm dedicated to large-scale technology buyouts. Back then, investors generally steered clear of tech firms; tech buyouts account for less than 1 percent of all U.S. acquisitions by value, according to Thomson Financial. But the four co-founders of Silver Lake saw an opportunity where others saw risk and complications. So, unlike most buyout firms (which lean toward diversification), Silver Lake placed all its eggs in one basket, gambling on technology and technology alone. So far, the group's wager has paid off. With annualized returns of nearly 22 percent on its first fund, Silver Lake earned its place among the crème de la crème in private equity. Further evidence of the group's success is the recent buyout of SunGard Data Systems. In August 2005, Silver Lake led a consortium of seven private equity firms to acquire SunGard for $11.3 billion, the largest technology deal every completed.

Mature market

These days, Silver Lake isn't the only one investing in tech companies. As the company predicted, the technology market has matured and offers a veritable feast for buyout companies. Tech companies with cash flow, predictable sales and single-digit growth are, if not quite a dime a dozen, certainly in greater abundance than they were when Silver Lake was getting started. Furthermore, because a steady stream of cash usually translates to timely loan payments, banks are more willing to make loans than they used to be. And increased borrowing power means bigger buyout deals – in the realm of $10 to $20 billion.

Hands-on

Once Silver Lake invests in a company, it pursues a very hands-on approach. The partners team up with management teams to make improvements in key business areas, including strategic planning and corporate development, organizational design, recruiting, customer and partner relationship development, sales and marketing, media and public relations, and capital markets and investor relations. Silver Lake calls on a team of 23 investment professionals working out of offices in Menlo Park, New York and London. Its senior partners boast more than 20 years of experience in the finance, investment and technology industries. The private equity group is also associated with investment firm Integral Capital Partners and venture capital firm Kleiner Perkins Caufield & Byers.

On the horizon

In April 2004, Silver Lake closed its second fund with committed capital of $3.6 billion. New investments for the tech private equity group include Sniffer Technologies, the network and application performance management business of Network Associates; integrated solutions provider Thomson; Instinet's Institutional Broker division; and the semiconductor products business of Agilent Technologies. For this last deal, Silver Lake partnered with Kohlberg Kravis Roberts (KKR) to bid $2.65 billion, beating out rivals Texas Pacific Group and Francisco Partners. Insiders say the new owners are likely to focus on Agilent's personal business (chips for mobile phones, printers, consumer electronics and the like) and may spin off Agilent's networking business (chips for fiber-optic equipment and computer storage devices). Sources also hypothesize that Silver Lake may be looking abroad in the coming months. Silver Lake already has an office in London, and in June 2005, the firm hired Asia expert and former head of IBM Global Services, John Joyce.

GETTING HIRED

Silver Lake Partners does not offer any career information on its web site. The best bet for candidates interested in working for the private equity group is to contact one of the firm's offices directly.

Visit Vault at **www.vault.com** for insider company profiles, expert advice, career message boards, expert resume reviews, the Vault Job Board and more.

VAULT CAREER LIBRARY

93

Summit Partners

222 Berkeley Street
18th Floor
Boston, MA 02116
Phone: (617) 824-1000
Fax: (617) 824-1100
www.summitpartners.com

THE STATS

Managing Partner: Bruce R. Evans
Employer Type: Private Company
No. of Employees: 110+
No. of Offices: 3

KEY COMPETITORS

Bain Capital
TA Associates

EMPLOYMENT CONTACT

See the "careers" page at
www.summitpartners.com

THE SCOOP

Sky's the limit for Summit

Over the course of its 21-year history, Summit Partners has become one of the largest U.S. private equity and venture capital firms. Since its founding in 1984 by two former TA Associates veterans, the Boston-based Summit has raised approximately $9 billion in capital and invested in more than 270 businesses, which together have completed over 100 public offerings and 100 strategic sales or mergers. The firm makes private equity, venture capital and subordinated debt investments of $5 million to more than $500 million per company. However, its focus on late-stage, profitable growth investments places Summit somewhere between a venture firm and a buyout shop.

Summit has over 110 employees and its 14 partners have more than 200 years of private equity and venture capital experience, averaging 15 years per partner. The firm's portfolio companies operate in a wide range of industries, including software, communications and technology, semiconductors and electronics, information services, financial services, business services, health care and life sciences, industrial products and consumer products. In addition to its headquarters in Boston, Summit has offices in Palo Alto and London.

The early years

Summit Partners was founded in 1984 by Stephen Woodsum and E. Roe Stamps, both long-time employees of Boston-based venture firm TA Associates and experienced technology and health care investors; they had also previously worked together at First Chicago Investment Corp. Like TA, Summit was created as a firm that rode the line between a venture firm and buyout shop, putting its money into high-growth companies. Summit's first fund closed in 1985. The firm raised $160 million, $100 million of which came from an investor group headed by Shearson/American Express, the balance from French banks and tech companies.

Funded

In June 2005, Summit Partners closed two private funds. The $3 billion Summit Partners Private Equity Fund VII will make investments from $25 million to $450 million, and the $300 million Summit Partners Venture Capital Fund II will make investments from $5 million to $25 million. According to the firm, the funds will be

Visit Vault at www.vault.com for insider company profiles, expert advice,
career message boards, expert resume reviews, the Vault Job Board and more.

VAULT CAREER LIBRARY   95

used to invest in growing, profitable, privately held later-stage companies in North America and Europe in a broad range of industries.

Blurring the line

The line between private equity and hedge funds is becoming hazier by the minute, as firms from both worlds begin to dabble in each others investments. In August 2005, for example, Summit Partners invested $127 million in the $5 billion hedge fund Coast Asset Management in one of the first major stakes in a hedge fund by a private equity firm. Experts wonder whether the plethora of hedge fund deals as of late (others include JPMorgan's purchase of a majority stake in Highbridge Capital Management and Legg Mason's acquisition of Permal Group) is a sign that hedge funds have peaked. But David Smith, the chief executive of Coast, says the firm chose to sell a minority stake because it remains bullish about growth opportunities. Smith also indicated that Coast would use its partnership with Summit to buy other hedge fund firms.

Other recent deals include a $6 million minority investment in MDVIP, the Boca Raton, Fla.-based concierge medicine leader in the U.S.; a $76 million majority stake in Actix Limited, the leading provider of wireless performance engineering solutions; and a majority position in Aramsco Inc., an environment supply company.

Top of the charts

Summit's portfolio companies have received some honors recently. In 2004, *The Deal* ranked the firm's investment in Jamba! AG European private equity deal of the year. The award was based on "successful executions resulting in exits at rich multiples." In September 2003, Summit invested $40 million in equity in Jamba!, a Berlin-based wireless digital content company. Less than a year later, in May 2004, Summit sold Jamba! to VeriSign, Inc. for $273 million, booking a return of 3.8 times its investment.

Additionally, World Wide Technology Holding Co., another of Summit's portfolio companies, won the top ranking on *Black Enterprise* magazine's 2004 list of highest-grossing black-owned businesses in the industrial/services category for the second year in a row. Summit invested in Telcobuy in 2000 and later assisted in its merger with WWT Holding.

TA Associates

High Street Tower, Suite 2500
125 High Street
Boston, MA 02110
Phone: (617) 574-6700
Fax: (617) 574-6728
www.ta.com

THE STATS

CEO: C. Kevin Landry
Employer Type: Private Company
No. of Employees: 40+
No. of Offices: 4

KEY COMPETITORS

Bain Capital
J.W. Childs
Summit Partners

EMPLOYMENT CONTACT

careers@ta.com

Visit Vault at **www.vault.com** for insider company profiles, expert advice,
career message boards, expert resume reviews, the Vault Job Board and more.

V/\ULT CAREER LIBRARY

97

THE SCOOP

Cold callers

Founded in 1968, TA Associates got its start as part of the Tucker Anthony investment bank. The unit was spun off in 1978, and in 1990, under the direction of current chief executive Kevin Landry, it decided to forego its venture capital business and concentrate exclusively on later-stage leveraged buyouts. Although TA may have shifted its focus over the years, it hasn't changed its primary strategy: the cold call. Through cold calling, the company has compiled a database of some 280,000 companies, and each year, its associates add another 8,000 to the list. From this vast catalog of companies, TA chooses to visit some 800 companies annually and invests in just a fraction of those. To date, TA has invested $3.5 billion in more than 350 companies; in 2004 alone, it invested $700 million in 12 companies. In total, the firm manages some $6 billion in assets, with typical investments ranging from around $25 million to $300 million.

Risky business

Back in 1990, TA Associates had about 85 companies in its portfolio, some of which were losing money – and absorbing all of the firm's time. "We were in the business of free consulting to struggling companies," Landry told *Boston Business Journal* in November 2004, "and that's probably not a very good business." That year (1990) was when TA opted to give up venture capital and focus on more established businesses. Said Landry of the decision, "We found that there was a correlation between reward and risk – but that correlation was that the less risk we took, the greater the reward. They don't teach you that in business school!"

Still, Landry isn't completely risk-averse. When associates clamored for a piece of the Internet market in late 1999, Landry relented —even though Internet start-ups went against the firm's target profile. Luckily for TA, Landry put an end to Internet investments in March 2000, right as the Internet bubble burst.

"Fintech"

Although TA Associates is willing to consider investments in almost any industry, the firm has expertise in the areas of technology, financial and business services, health care and consumer industries. The private equity group has also built up a portfolio of what TA calls "fintech" companies, those that blend finance and technology. Two of the firm's most prominent "fintech" investments are electronic trading companies Instinet and Ameritrade. TA is Instinet's largest minority stockholder, with a stake of about 4 percent, and Ameritrade's third largest institutional investor, with a claim to around 4.7 percent. Lower profile "fintech" investments include GlobeOp Financial Services and Intercontinental Exchange Inc.

London calling

Based in Boston, TA Associates has offices in Menlo Park, Pittsburgh and London. Its London office is its most recent endeavor, opened in 2003 as a two-man shop led by principal Ajit Nedungadi. In March 2005, Christian Grunwald joined the London team as a vice president, bringing the outpost's staff to four. Grunwald brings five years of private equity experience to the table and comes to TA Associates from General Atlantic Partners in Düsseldorf. Grunwald also spent time with McKinsey & Company in Zurich and with Roland Berger in Munich and Madrid.

Succession matters

TA Associates is Kevin Landry's only white collar job. Landry has been with the firm since its inception, when founder Peter Brooke hired Landry fresh out of University of Pennsylvania's Wharton School. Since then, Landry has risen to become the firm's chief executive officer, the face of TA Associates and the "cold-call captain." Although Landry is still around to close deals, he doesn't seek them out anymore and looks forward to slowing down. The CEO expects to retire (or at least reduce his responsibilities) in early 2006 after TA closes its 10th fund. Experts say Landry's departure won't be an issue for TA Associates, which has built a brand that will survive succession.

GETTING HIRED

Individuals interested in working for TA Associates should check out the careers section of the company web site. The private equity firm offers an associate program for college graduates with one to two years of investment banking, consulting or other relevant deal experience. Associates at TA can expect to work closely with managing directors to find, analyze and finance new private equity deals. But getting a job at TA isn't easy. In 2004, the firm interviewed 100 job seekers for around seven entry-level positions. Candidates for this program and other careers with TA

Visit Vault at **www.vault.com** for insider company profiles, expert advice, career message boards, expert resume reviews, the Vault Job Board and more.

VAULT CAREER LIBRARY

99

Associates should send their resumes to careers@ta.com and indicate location preference.

Texas Pacific Group

301 Commerce Street, Suite 3300
Fort Worth, TX 76102
Phone: (817) 871-4000
Fax: (817) 871-4001

THE STATS

Managing Partners: David
Bonderman, Jim Coulter & Bill Price
Employer Type: Private Company
No. of Employees: 60+
No. of Offices: 3

KEY COMPETITORS

Hicks Muse
KKR
Thomas H. Lee Partners

EMPLOYMENT CONTACT

Phone: (817) 871-4000

Visit Vault at **www.vault.com** for insider company profiles, expert advice,
career message boards, expert resume reviews, the Vault Job Board and more.

VAULT CAREER LIBRARY   101

THE SCOOP

On a roll

Founded in 1993, Texas Pacific Group is a leading private equity with some $15 million in assets under management and 65 transactions under its belt. These days, say insiders, the firm is bigger and busier than ever. Of late, TPG has partnered with other firms to buy luxury retailer Neiman Marcus; a stake in Lenovo Group, China's largest computer maker; and SunGard Data Systems, in the largest LBO since the RJR Nabisco buyout in 1989. Early in 2004, the company closed its fourth fund at $5.8 billion, a significant landmark for TPG considering it launched its first fund in 1993 with $720 million.

Evolution

In the past, Texas Pacific Group has pursued distressed companies, the ones other investors wouldn't get anywhere near – think Burger King. But these days, more than half of the group's capital goes toward high-quality, low-risk investments such as SunGard, Neiman Marcus and Petco Animal Supplies. Although in the past TPG has focused on investments in technology (Seagate Technology), consumer products (Ducati), retail (J. Crew) and airlines (Continental), the firm is branching out with deals in media (MGM) and energy (Texas Genco Holdings).

Greek to me

Although, as its name indicates, Texas Pacific Group is based in the Lone Star State, the private equity group is no ingénue when it comes to the rest of the world. The firm has an additional U.S. office in San Francisco, a European outpost in London and an affiliate in Asia (called Newbridge Capital). In fact, TPG was one of the first major U.S. private equity firms to establish a European business; past transactions include Ducati Motor, Punch Taverns, Scottish & Newcastle Retail and Findexa. In 2003, Texas Pacific Group won Thomson's European buyout deal of the year for its acquisition of U.K. retailer Debenhams for £1.7 billion. The firm's takeover of Greek telecommunications company TIM Hellas is the group's most recent European deal. In April 2005, TPG and Apax Partners announced the acquisition of TIM Hellas for €1.1 billion.

More hits than misses

When you take a gamble on down-and-out companies, you're bound to have some misses from time to time. Texas Pacific is no exception. Low-achievers for the firm include Gate Gourmet Group, Bally, Ducati Motor and ON Semiconductor. But in 2004, TPG and another private equity group sold off Petco for a gain of nearly six times their initial investment of $190 million just four years earlier. And Burger King, with new chief executive George Brenneman, looks like a success story in the making. Brenneman reported that by mid-2005, the franchise had already earned more money than it had in all of 2004. Furthermore, Texas Pacific's third fund has been delivering internal rates of return of around 16 percent, well above expected returns of 11 percent.

GETTING HIRED

Texas Pacific Group does not have a web site. Candidates interested in learning more about job opportunities with TPG should contact the firm directly at its headquarters in Fort Worth, Tex.

Visit Vault at **www.vault.com** for insider company profiles, expert advice, career message boards, expert resume reviews, the Vault Job Board and more.

VAULT CAREER LIBRARY 103

Thoma Cressey Equity Partners

Sears Tower
92nd Floor
233 South Wacker Drive
Chicago, IL 60606
Phone: (312) 777-4444
Fax: (312) 777-4445
www.thomacressey.com

THE STATS

Co-founders: Bryan C. Cressey &
Carl D. Thoma
Employer Type: Private Company
Revenue: $8.6 million (FYE 12/04)
No. of Employees: 31
No. of Offices: 3

EMPLOYMENT CONTACT

Boston: (617) 367-3000
Chicago: (312) 777-4444
San Francisco: (415) 263-3660

THE SCOOP

Buy and build

In the 1980s, the prevailing buyout strategy was buy and bust; private equity firms would acquire a distressed company and break it up into pieces. By the 1990s, a new and friendlier approach had taken center stage, a tactic known as "platform investing," "leveraged buildup" or, less technically, "buy and build." This new methodology was pioneered by Golder, Thoma, Cressey, Rauner (GTCR), the predecessor to Thoma Cressey Equity Partners. Although the latter didn't get its start until 1998, when GTCR split into two separate firms, Thoma Cressey traces its roots back to 1980 and its partners boast an average of more than 15 years of experience.

To date, Thoma Cressey and its predecessor have invested more than $2 billion through seven funds in around 80 companies, with a typical investment in the range of $20 to $100 million. The buyout group specializes in four main sectors – consumer products and services, health care, software and business services – and limits its investments to companies headquartered in the U.S. and Canada. The firm's 31 employees work out of offices in Boston, Chicago and San Francisco.

Dynamic duo

Thoma Cressey Equity Partners was founded by Carl D. Thoma and Bryan C. Cressey. A native of Oklahoma, Thoma received his BS from Oklahoma State University in 1970 and his MBA from Stanford in 1973. Just seven years later, after a brief stint with First Chicago Equity Group, Thoma joined forces with Cressey and another partner, Stanley Golder, to establish Golder, Thoma & Co (which later became Golder, Thoma, Cressey, Rauner). Cressey earned his undergraduate degree at the University of Washington and his MBA and JD at Harvard University. An expert in the health care services field, Cressey also began his career at First Chicago Equity Group.

Care-ful investments

In December 2004, Thoma Cressey acquired a majority stake in Continuing Care Rx, a provider of pharmacy services to nursing homes and prisons. The private equity group hopes to boost the company's sales by picking up market share from bigger competitors, which often fail to deliver prescriptions on time, and by making strategic acquisitions. The buyout group undoubtedly hopes to repeat its success with

Visit Vault at www.vault.com for insider company profiles, expert advice, career message boards, expert resume reviews, the Vault Job Board and more.

VAULT CAREER LIBRARY   105

Critical Care Systems, Inc. Thoma Cressey quintupled its $17 million investment in the pharmaceutical infusion services provider when it sold Critical Care Systems for $150 million in April 2004.

Another success story for Thoma Cressey is Prophet 21, a provider of vertical-market focused enterprise software and services for the distribution industry. In January 2003, the private equity group, together with LLR Partners, invested $40 million in the buyout of Prophet 21. The firms worked with the software company, doubling its customer base through a series of seven acquisitions and making it an attractive acquisition target. The strategy worked. In August 2005, Thoma Cressey and LLR sold the company to Activant Solutions, a provider of business management solutions, for $215 million.

GETTING HIRED

Thoma Cressey Equity Partners does not provide career information on its web site. Candidates should contact the firm directly at its offices in Boston, Chicago or San Francisco.

Thomas H. Lee Partners L.P.

100 Federal Street, 35th Floor
Boston, MA 02110
Phone: (617) 227-1050
Fax: (617) 227-3514

THE STATS

Chairman & CEO: Thomas H. Lee
Employer Type: Private Company
No. of Employees: 28
No. of Offices: 1

KEY COMPETITORS

Blackstone Group
Hicks Muse
KKR

EMPLOYMENT CONTACT

Phone: (617) 227-1050

Visit Vault at **www.vault.com** for insider company profiles, expert advice,
career message boards, expert resume reviews, the Vault Job Board and more.

VAULT CAREER LIBRARY   107

THE SCOOP

The friendly firm

At the age of 31, Thomas H. Lee Partners is one of the oldest private equity firms in the U.S. The Boston-based group also has a reputation for being one of the more friendly leverage buyout companies in the business, going after only those corporations that want to be taken over. As founder and chief executive of the eponymous firm, Thomas Lee told the *Daily Deal* in April 2005, "Everything our firm does is friendly. We like to go where we are wanted." The private equity group's targets are middle-market companies with short-term (three to five years) growth potential, acquired through a combination of debt, funds from institutional investors and its own money. Notable investments include Snapple Beverage, GNC and Houghton Mifflin. Thomas H. Lee currently has about $14 billion under management.

Asia Pacific ho!

In the past, Thomas H. Lee has focused on investments in the U.S. and Europe. In September 2005, however, the private equity group announced plans to team up with H&Q Asia Pacific. THL Partners will take advantage of H&Q Asia Pacific's established infrastructure, extensive network and long-standing presence in the region to pursue LBO opportunities in China, Japan and Korea, and to allow its portfolio companies to locate expansion and outsourcing opportunities in Asia.

Mega funds

Since 1984, Thomas H. Lee Partners has raised five funds, the last of which closed in 2001 at $6.1 billion. In June 2005, the private equity group said it plans to raise a new fund with a $7.5 billion target – just one of many mega funds in the current buyout market. The Carlyle Group, for example, just raised a $7.8 billion buyout fund, breaking the previous record. In this mega world, the new record is only expected to last as long as it takes the likes of Goldman Sachs, Blackstone and Warburg Pincus to get their fundraising efforts in line.

New deals

THL Partners typically considers around 1,000 deals per year, but invests in just three to four, usually committing $200 million to $600 million per transaction. Recent investments include Warner Chilcott, a pharmaceutical company specializing in women's health care and dermatology. In February 2005, THL Partners joined forces with Bain Capital Partners, DLJ Merchant Banking III and JPMorgan Partners to acquire Warner Chilcott for $3.1 billion. Just a month earlier, THL announced plans to sell Eye Care Centers of America (ECCA) to Moulin International Holdings Limited and Golden Gate Capital for $450 million. Insiders say THL Partners may be teaming up with Blackstone in a bid for the luxury retail chain Neiman Marcus Group, and has submitted an unsolicited $1.2 billion takeover offer for Callaway Golf, the nation's largest manufacturer of golf clubs.

GETTING HIRED

Boston-based Thomas H. Lee Partners doesn't have a web site. Individuals interested in working for the private equity group can try to contact the firm via telephone or check out financial job sites such as jobsinthemoney.com and glocap.com.

Visit Vault at **www.vault.com** for insider company profiles, expert advice,
career message boards, expert resume reviews, the Vault Job Board and more.

VAULT CAREER LIBRARY   109

TowerBrook Capital Partners, LP

430 Park Avenue
New York, NY 10022
Phone: (212) 699-2200
Fax: (917) 591-9851
www.towerbrook.com

THE STATS

Co-CEO (New York): Neal Moszkowski
Co-CEO (London): Ramez Sousou
Employer Type: Private Company
No. of Employees: 30
No. of Offices: 2

EMPLOYMENT CONTACT

New York: (212) 699-2200
London: +44 20 7451 2020

THE SCOOP

New name, same game

In April 2005, hedge fund group Soros Fund Management spun off its private equity division TowerBrook Capital Partners (formerly known as Soros Private Equity). While the firm may have a new name (and independence), nearly all of Soros' former employees, including co-heads Neal Moszkowski and Ramez Sousou, have joined TowerBrook. Like its predecessor, TowerBrook targets companies with strong cash flow and growth prospects, often seeking out distressed situations that present attractive investment opportunities. The firm partners with managers and calls on the expertise of its management advisory board (composed of experienced managers) to affect change.

All in the family

The spin-off of TowerBrook in April is part of a larger restructuring plan for former parent company Soros Fund Management. Back in October 2004, Soros founder and chairman George Soros, the billionaire financier and philanthropist, spun off the firm's real estate fund management team into Grove Capital and the firm's credit team into Dune Capital Management. At the same time, Soros set up his sons, Robert and Jonathan, in key positions to concentrate on the remaining hedge fund business. The older son Robert now heads the $8.3 billion Quantum Endowment Fund (the hedge fund division) and is deputy chief executive officer of Soros Fund Management. His younger brother Jonathan serves as co-deputy chief executive officer of Soros Fund Management.

Healthy investment

New York-based TowerBrook has approximately $1.3 billion under management and specializes in the health care, telecommunications, media, chemicals, utilities and energy sectors. Its portfolio includes college sports television network CSTV, WellCare Health Plans, Auto Europe, drug testing and background screening company DISA, and latex producer Polymer Latex.

The firm's investment in WellCare Health Plans, which provides managed care services to government-sponsored health care programs (Medicare and Medicaid), has made TowerBrook a lot of money. TowerBrook has turned its initial investment of $70 million (July 2002) into nearly $400 million. About six months after

Visit Vault at www.vault.com for insider company profiles, expert advice, career message boards, expert resume reviews, the Vault Job Board and more.

VAULT CAREER LIBRARY   111

WellCare's initial public offering in July 2004, TowerBrook sold some 5.6 million shares at $32 a piece, translating to $179.2 million. Then, in July 2005, the private equity group sold 6 million shares in a secondary offering, realizing an additional $202 million.

Money-makers

In another money-making move, TowerBrook returned twice the cost of its original investment in PolymerLatex – without selling the company. In June 2005, the private equity group refinanced PolymerLatex in a deal valued at $260 million. The proceeds will go toward the recapitalization of the company's debt and vendor loans – and toward a dividend for TowerBrook.

More recently, in September 2005, Liberty Global (headed and mostly owned by Denver cable mogul John Malone) announced it will pay $2.7 billion to acquire Cablecom, Switzerland's No. 2 cable company. TowerBrook, together with Apollo Management and Goldman Sachs, bought a 53 percent stake in Cablecom in 2003, and said the firm will make four times its initial outlay.

GETTING HIRED

TowerBrook does not provide career information on its web site. Individuals interested in working for TowerBrook should contact the firm directly at its offices in New York or London.

Veronis Suhler Stevenson Partners LLC

350 Park Avenue
New York, NY 10022
Phone: (212) 935-4990
www.vss.com

THE STATS

Chairman & Co-CEO: John J. Veronis
President & Co-CEO: John S. Suhler
Co-CEO: Jeffrey Stevenson
Employer Type: Private company
No. of Employees: 80
No. of Offices: 2

KEY COMPETITORS

Allen & Company
Boston Ventures

EMPLOYMENT CONTACT

Director of Human Resources
Veronis Suhler Stevenson
350 Park Avenue
New York, New York 10022
See "careers" at www.vss.com

Visit Vault at **www.vault.com** for insider company profiles, expert advice,
career message boards, expert resume reviews, the Vault Job Board and more.

VAULT CAREER LIBRARY 113

THE SCOOP

Betting on the media

Veronis Suhler Stevenson, a private equity and mezzanine capital fund management firm, invests in the media, communications and information industries in North America and Europe. The firm also provides investment banking advisory services to media companies, consulting firms on mergers and acquisitions, helping firms raise equity and debt, performing fairness opinions and valuations, and providing industry research.

Veronis Suhler's private equity investments are conducted through its VS&A Communications Partners subsidiaries, which oversee individual funds for investment in its three target industries. The firm currently has two private equity funds in existence, the $330 million VS&A Communications Partners II, L.P. and the $1 billion VS&A Communications Partners III, L.P. The firm's first fund, VS&A Communications Partners, L.P., was formed with $57 million of capital in 1987 and has since been liquidated; during its existence, the fund yielded an annual return (45 percent) high enough to put it among the top acquisition funds started in the late 1980s. In January 2004, Veronis Suhler raised $100 million for the firm's first mezzanine fund, VSS Mezzanine Partners L.P., which will provide subordinated debt primarily to middle-market companies for use in acquisitions and recapitalizations.

Since 1987, Veronis Suhler has managed over $2 billion in committed capital. The firm invests in buyouts, recapitalizations, growth financings and strategic acquisitions. To date, its equity funds have invested in 34 platform companies, which have closed more than 185 add-on acquisitions, resulting in a portfolio with realized and unrealized values of $7.5 billion. Some of the firm's investments include Hanley-Wood, Ascend Media, Facts On File and Hemscott.

Making money on media

In 1981, publishing industry veterans John J. Veronis and John S. Suhler founded Veronis Suhler, a financial services firm catering solely to the media, communications and information industries. Veronis was best known for starting *Psychology Today*, while Suhler had been president of CBS Publishing Group, through which he oversaw various book publishing houses and well-known magazines such as *Woman's Day*, *Field & Stream* and *Road & Track*. Jeffrey Stevenson joined the bank in 1982 and became a name partner in 2000. Today,

Veronis Suhler Stevenson offers M&A and financing advisory, private equity investing and industry research. The firm has offices in New York and London.

Big in banking, too

Like the successful careers of its founders, Veronis Suhler has been built upon a combination of financial know-how and industry expertise; the firm's private equity employees and investment bankers have been plucked from such firms as JPMorgan, Merrill Lynch, Time Warner, NBC and Times Mirror. Utilizing their industry knowledge, Veronis Suhler employees work in teams concentrating on particular media segments, including broadcasting, newspaper publishing and the Internet. Along with its work in the private equity arena, the firm's bankers have been busy, too. Since its inception, Veronis Suhler has worked on more than 650 investment banking advisory transactions.

Informing the information industry

In 2004, the firm consolidated its two comprehensive industry research reports, "The Communications Industry Forecast" and "The Communications Industry Report," into "The Communications Industry Forecast," which analyzes spending patterns and the major drivers impacting growth in the media and communications industry. "The Communications Industry Report" discusses the financial results of every public company in the media and communications industry. And to keep its own employees current on market happenings, Veronis Suhler supplies an internal publication, the "Veronis Suhler Stevenson Market Report," which offers weekly industry updates.

GETTING HIRED

On the "careers" section of its web site, the firm posts open private equity positions, accompanied by an extensive list of requirements. In the past, professionals have been tapped for spots at VSS from major banks and investment firms, as well as from companies such as Time Warner, Hachette Filipacchi and CBS. Candidates can e-mail employment questions to recruiting@vss.com, or send a resume and cover letter, including salary history, to the Director of Human Resources at the Park Avenue address.

Visit Vault at **www.vault.com** for insider company profiles, expert advice, career message boards, expert resume reviews, the Vault Job Board and more.

VAULT CAREER LIBRARY   115

Welsh, Carson, Anderson & Stowe

320 Park Ave., Ste. 2500
New York, NY 10022-6815
Phone: 212-893-9500
Fax: 212-893-9575
www.welshcarson.com

DEPARTMENTS*

Communications
Health Care
Information & Business Services

*Focus industries

THE STATS

General Partner, Information & Business Services: Bruce K. Anderson
General Partner, Health Care: Russell Lloyd Carson
General Partner, Information & Business Services: Patrick J. Welsh
Employer Type: Private company
No. of Offices: 1

KEY COMPETITORS

Clayton, Dubilier & Rice
Platinum Equity
Willis Stein

EMPLOYMENT CONTACT

320 Park Avenue
Suite 2500
New York, New York 10022-6815
Phone: (212) 893-9500
Fax: (212) 893-9575

THE SCOOP

Three-industry firm

Since its founding in 1979, the private equity firm Welsh, Carson, Anderson & Stowe has organized 13 limited partnerships with total capital of more than $12 billion, making it one of the largest in the U.S. The firm is currently investing equity from Welsh, Carson, Anderson & Stowe IX, L.P., a $3.8 billion equity fund, and WCAS Capital Partners IV, L.P., a $1.3 billion dedicated subordinated debt fund. It typically invests between $50 million and $500 million in a company, often holding a controlling interest.

Welsh Carson focuses on investing in three industries: information and business services, health care and, to a lesser extent, communications. The firm invests in growth companies then builds value through internal growth and acquisitions. According to Welsh Carson, it's the largest private equity investor in both the information and business services and health care sectors.

Indeed, the firm has an impressive track record in these industries, having helped create several industry-leading companies. According to the firm, "There are 34 public companies in [its] primary industries with a total market capitalization exceeding $100 billion that can trace their roots in some meaningful way to [Welsh Carson]." A few of these include Alliance Data Systems Corporation, SunGard Data Systems and The BISYS Group in the information and business services industry, and Lincare Holdings, Select Medical Corporation and United Surgical Partners in health care.

To date, the firm has invested in more than 135 companies in its target industries and funded over 650 follow-on acquisitions. The firm's current portfolio claims 22 companies with combined revenue of $14 billion and EBITDA (earnings before interest, tax, depreciation and amortization) of $3 billion. Investors in the firm's funds have included public and private pension funds, banks, insurance companies, university endowments and other institutional investors. Welsh Carson's portfolio companies include Ruesch International, US Investigations Services, BancTec, Global Knowledge Network, Valor Telecommunications, Savvis Communications, Onward Healthcare, US Oncology, and Accuro Healthcare Solutions.

Namesakes

Co-founder Patrick J. Welsh focuses on investments in the information and business services industry. Prior to co-founding the firm in 1979, Welsh spent eight years with Citicorp Venture Capital; he was president there when he left. Welsh graduated from Rutgers University and received an MBA from UCLA. Russel L. Carson, another co-founder, focuses on health care investments. Prior to co-founding the firm, Carson was chairman and CEO of Citicorp Venture Capital. Carson holds an undergraduate degree from Dartmouth and an MBA from Columbia. Like Welsh, firm co-founder Bruce K. Anderson focuses on investments in the information and business services industry. Anderson previously spent nine years at Automatic Data Processing where he was executive vice president, president of ADP International and a member of the board of directors. Anderson graduated from the University of Minnesota in 1962.

Sub debt as well

The firm's subordinated debt funds can reduce the time of capital raising, insulating Welsh Carson from the uncertainties of the public debt markets and allowing the firm to structure transactions with businesses or divisions that cannot access public debt markets. Its fourth subordinated debt fund, WCAS Capital Partners IV, L.P., closed in November 2004. Total capital commitments to the fund equaled $1.3 billion

GETTING HIRED

The firm does not list open positions or post career information on its web site. To find out about possible openings, contact the firm via telephone at (212) 893-4500.

About the Author

Derek Loosvelt is a graduate of the Wharton School at the University of Pennsylvania. He is a writer and editor and has worked for *Brill's Content* and Inside.com. Previously, he worked in investment banking at CIBC and Duff & Phelps.

Visit Vault at **www.vault.com** for insider company profiles, expert advice, career message boards, expert resume reviews, the Vault Job Board and more.

V∧ULT CAREER LIBRARY   119

Competition on the Street – and beyond – is heating up. With the finance job market tightening, you need to be your best.

We know the finance industry. And we've got experts that know the finance environment standing by to review your resume and give you the boost you need to snare the financial position you deserve.

Finance Resume Writing and Resume Reviews

- Have your resume reviewed by a practicing finance professional.

- For resume writing, start with an e-mailed history and 1- to 2-hour phone discussion. Our experts will write a first draft, and deliver a final draft after feedback and discussion.

- For resume reviews, get an in-depth, detailed critique and rewrite within TWO BUSINESS DAYS.

Finance Career Coaching

Have a pressing finance career situation you need Vault's expert advice with? We've got experts who can help.

- Trying to get into investment banking from business school or other careers?

- Switching from one finance sector to another – for example, from commercial banking to investment banking?

- Trying to figure out the cultural fit of the finance firm you should work for?

"Thank you, thank you, thank you! I would have never come up with these changes on my own!"
– *W.B., Associate, Investment Banking, NY*

"Having an experienced pair of eyes looking at the resume made more of a difference than I thought."
– *R.T., Managing Director, SF*

"I found the coaching so helpful I made three appointments!"
– *S.B., Financial Planner, NY*

For more information go to www.vault.com/finance

VAULT
> the most trusted name in career information™